First Edition 2013

Oliver Cameron Publishing
Maidstone
Kent
UK

www.oliver-cameron.com
www.triathlon-questions.com

MW00747960

Edited by Janet Goode

ISBN 978-0956546371

Thank you to Sarah and James for putting up with me, my regular travels and my bike purchases. I really do appreciate it even if I don't always show it. And James - you will be able to race very soon yourself if you can drag yourself away from your guitar!

Thank you to all members of the Maidstone Harriers and in particular the Triathlon section - you are all a sense of inspiration to me.

Thank you to Graeme Kelly for some great battles - twice separated in triathlons by just 2 seconds. Long may it continue and I hope your fantastic new Tri bike does not make you too fast!

Thank you to Sarah "The Machine" Brenton for going so fast it taught me to push myself to the limit and suffer to try and keep up with you.

Thank you to Janet Goode for editing the vast majority of this text - you have done a marvelous job.

Thank you to Andy, Amy and Chenin for inviting me into your home in beautiful Umbria to train, write and get some warm weather.

"Yesterday was reality, today is opportunity and tomorrow is your destiny"

David Pearce
2008

Introduction

A friend of mine (Michael White) who has completed a number of Triathlons recently commented that "No matter how I feel before a race, when it's all over I find my enthusiasm for the sport just increases". I think this sums triathlon up perfectly. There is no doubt that Triathlon takes time to train in 3 disciplines and you have to make sacrifices but the pleasure you get from that training and racing gives an immense sense of achievement. Triathlon to me seems to be so much more "inclusive" than swimming, cycling and running individually. There is a camaraderie at races between everyone, that is not so evident in the other sports. I think this is gained by the fact we do not just register and then race, we have to prepare in transition providing the opportunity to chat with others before and after the race.

Triathlon is also highly inspirational. Only yesterday, having finished my first triathlon of the season, I stood in awe and watched some of the final competitors finishing. Due to the nature of shorter races (with a pool swim), start times are staggered meaning the slowest person on the course could finish almost at the same time as the actual winner which I love. It takes away the fear of being last as no one knows your time and you are not alone on the course.

The public have a vision of triathletes being young, super skinny and fit when in reality a race contains people of all ages, sizes and abilities. I love the fact that so many women are competing (and beating me easily) which makes for a far better race. At a guess, based on observation, the majority of competitors are over 30 with some in their 70's still going strong.

To me the appeal is the participation in three disciplines. If you are not strong in one you have another two to excel in. This evens things up a little between friends, especially if one prefers cycling and another running. In my Tri Club (Maidstone Harriers) I look forward to each season and my battles with Graeme, Sarah, Paul, Richard, Penny, Sharon and Michael as we all seem to have times within a few minutes of each other, making for some great racing. In fact Graeme and I have each beaten each other by exactly 2 seconds in our last 2 triathlons which I find incredible. When racing is this close it makes it unbelievably exciting.

I am not an expert, professional and nor am I involved in Triathlon in anyway except as a competitor that hopes to come in the top 25% of the field. This was not always the case though, I used to be overweight and finish in the bottom 10% but have improved through training and experience. I was just as happy finishing last as my sense of accomplishment was to have finished and be able to call myself a triathlete. Now that sense comes from competing against my friends and trying to improve on previous years times on the same course.

As you improve you will no doubt want to do a long distance triathlon consisting of a 3.8km swim, 180km bike and 42km run. This is my next challenge and one that I am looking forward to. I have progressed from finishing almost last in a Sprint Triathlon to be ready to compete in the Bolton Ironman in just 3 years. I have an enormous sense of pride in this and can't wait for race day to come.

I have written this book as I, and so many people that I speak too, have an abundance of questions about the sport that they would like answers too. Other books exist but you have to read through a lot of information to find what you want. In this book every question is listed at the front enabling you to find the answer easily. I wanted to list all the questions anyone coming into the sport or improving would have, simply to make life easy for them. I remember that it took me a good 6 months to know what an "Age Grouper" or a "Masters" swim session was (along with lots of questions about triathlon itself) as I felt foolish not knowing the answer and did not want to ask.

Although I have written the book myself, I have asked a number of experts in their specific field to review what I have written and to make any corrections they deemed necessary. The only exception is the injury chapter which was written completely by Mark Dayson as I did not know the answers and it is vital to give a educated and qualified answer.

As with all sports, please do contact your Doctor before taking up physical activity to make sure it is safe to do so. Even if you are fit, it is advised to have a heart check for cardiomyopathy etc.

All the advice given is from personal experience and you follow it at your own risk.

To keep up to date with special offers on gear and read reviews on new products please subscribe to our newsletter at www.triathlon-questions.com

David Pearce

P.S. Please "Like" our Facebook page to ask new questions, receive free training advice and keep up to date:- www.facebook.com/triathlonquestions

The Questions

General Questions
1. What are the various distances for triathlon?
2 .Why would I train and enter a triathlon?
3. I would love to do a triathlon but it costs a lot of money - what can I do?
4. Will I come last?
5. How hard is it to do a Triathlon?
6. What is an Age Grouper?
7. How am I timed?
8. Do men and women start together?
9. Does everyone start at the same time?
10. Is there a time limit for everyone to fnish?
11. Am I too old to do Triathlon?
12. Are bikes and helmets provided for a race?
13. Can I listen to my MP3 player?
14. Do I need any special clothes?
15. How do I !nd the time to train for 3 sports when I barely have enough time to train for one?
16. How do I fnd the time to train with my home life?
18. Are there any Tri Clubs local to me that take beginners?
19. Is it worth joining my region's Triathlon governing body?
20. Are there relay races?
21. Can I still drink alcohol whilst training?
22. Can I wear my surfng wetsuit?
23. Do I need a Heart Rate Monitor (HRM)?
24. Do I need a GPS watch?
25. Do I need compression clothes?
26. Do I need padding in my shorts?
27. Do I really have to go and train outside when it is freezing cold and blowing a gale?
28. Do I really need technical sportswear or can I make do with my t-shirts?
29. How do I carry my gels/bars etc?
30. What bars or gels should I use?
31. How can I find out what it is like to race, without racing?
32. How can I predict when I will reach the peak of my fitness?
33. How do I attach my race number to my t-shirt or expensive tri suit?

34. How do I stop chaffing?
35. How early should I arrive at my event?
36. Warming up seems like such a waste of time. Do I really have to do it?
37. How do I warm up?
38. I am a bit obsessive and like to train like a demon. Is this bad?
39. I am quite small and my wetsuit's arms and legs are too long. What can I do?
40. I have skipped training for a week - is it a disaster?
41. I know that sleep is important but what can I do to get a better night's sleep?
42. I really don't enjoy the training - what can I do?
43. I want to use sun screen but when I sweat it runs into my eyes. What can I do?
44. If I am doing a lake swim, will there be lifeguards?
45. Is it advisable to wear sunglasses even when it is overcast?
46. Is one thick top better than layering thinner ones for cold weather training?
47. I am a man and really do not like the idea of wearing "tights". Do I have too?
48. Should I have a race plan?
49. Should I buy my new kit at the event where there might be some good deals on?
50. Should I go straight into a Standard distance Tri or enter a Sprint Tri first?
51. Should I recce the transition area and swim locations?
52. Should I take a warm top to put on after the race?
53. Should I train on specific skills?
54. What do I keep my race kit in?
55. What do I wear?
56. Should I wear underwear?
57. What training time goals should I set myself?
58. What race time goals should I set myself?
59. What is the correct pace to race at?
60. What happens at registration?
61. What intensity should I train at?
62. What is a brick session?
63. What is periodisation?
64. What is the best way to get the really sticky race number off my bike?

65. What is the best way to recover after hard training to prepare me for the next session?
66. What is the most important aspect of training?
67. What is the number one rookie mistake when racing?
68. Which way around does a wetsuit suit go on?
69. Will there be enough toilets at the race for everyone to use?
70. How do I go to the toilet if I need to go?
71. What is a race belt?
72. What is a dismount line?
73. Do I need to have insurance?
74. What are XTerra races?
75. How do I choose a gym to join?
76. Should I drink lots of water the night before a race?
77. I see lots of Acronyms in !tness magazines – can you explain them please?
78. What do I do with all the medals I am going to get?

Swimming
79. What is the basic equipment required for swimming?
80. I am a bit ashamed of my body - can I wear a top in the swim?
81. What is a Masters swim session?
82. Do I need to be able to dive for a pool swim or do you start in the water?
83. Do I need to be able to tumble turn or do you just touch the side and go?
84. Are you able to overtake someone in the pool if you are much faster or do you have to wait until you get to the end of that length?
85. I am not very good at swimming - is this a problem?
86. Can I swim breast stroke?
87. Can I swim backstroke.
88. Do I need to be able to tumble turn or do you just touch the side and go?
89. I swim in the fast lane but there are some really slow people there - what can I do?
90. What are swimming drills and their benefits?
91. What happens if you touch the foot of the person in front of you and they don't let you past at the end of the length?
92. I am a little scared of open water - what happens if I have a panic attack?
93. Do I have to wear a wetsuit?

94. How can I get into my wetsuit more easily?
95. How can I get out of my wetsuit quickly?
96. Can I trim the legs and arms of my wetsuit?
97. When do I take my wetsuit off?
98. How do I cope if the lake water is very cold?
99. Should I bother to kick during my open water swim?
100. How do I see where I am going in an open water swim?
101. If I get hit in the swim what should I do?
102. I am worried that lakes are dirty and not healthy to swim in?
103. Will I be able to see underwater in an open water swim?
104. Will I come into contact with fish?
105. Will I be swam over?
106. What is drafting?
107. What is the best way to get around a Buoy when in open water?
108. What do I do if take in a big mouthful of lake or sea water?
109. What happens if my goggles get knocked off in the swim?
110. When do I take my goggles off after a wet suit swim?
111. What colour lenses should I have in my swim goggles?
112. How should my ankle be when swimming?
113. I have a hairy chest/back/arms/legs - should I shave?
114. Should I wear a swim hat?
115. Should my body be static or rotate in the swim?
116. Should my toes almost touch when kicking in the swim?
117. What is a pull when swimming?
118. What is over gliding?
119. What is bilateral breathing?
120. What is the catch when swimming?
121. What is the recovery when swimming?
122. What shape should I be in the water?
123. I always really smell of chlorine after a swim session. How can I eliminate this before work?
124. Do I need to drink during pool training?
125. How do I prepare myself when nearing the end of the swim to be able to run to transition?
126. What is a good target time to swim 400 metres?
127. What happens when you get out of the water – do you literally jump on the bike soaking wet?
128. How do I get faster on the swim?

Cycling

129. Can I ride my mountain bike?
130. How can I make my mountain bike faster?
131. When should I buy a road bike?
132. How much should I spend on a road bike?
133. Where is the best place to buy a used race bike?
134. Isn't cycling dangerous?
135. Do I have to wear a bike helmet?
136. Do I need a bike computer?
137. Do I need a Heart Rate Monitor?
138. Do I need a Women's speci!c road bike?
139. Do I ride my bike in the same clothes that I swim in?
140. Is it ok to use a bike at the gym or a turbo trainer at home?
141. What are clipless pedals?
142. Do I need clipless pedals?
143. Are clipless pedals scary to use?
144. What are Cleats?
145. Are there any gears I should not use?
146. How do I know when to change my chain and rear cassette?
147. Do deep rim or disk wheels make a difference?
148. Do I need a power meter?
149. Do I need to wear eyewear when cycling?
150. Do tri bars make a huge difference?
151. Should I count the carbohydrate content in my drink with my total
152. How do I get faster on the bike?
153. How do I prepare myself when nearing the end of the bike to be able to run?
154. How do I push my bike to the mount line efficiently?
155. How do I rack my bike?
156. Is my bike safe left on the racking?
157. When do I take my bike off the rack?
158. How do I stop getting cold/wet feet on the bike during winter?
159. How can I corner more efficiently and faster?
160. How will I remember where I have left my bike?
161. I am nervous on my bike when on the road - what can I do?
162. I am rubbish at climbing hills on a bike - what can I do?
163. What are hill reps?
164. My gears slip on my bike - are they broken?
165. Should I add integrated aero bars or clip on aero bars to my road

bike?

166. Do I need Aero Bars?
167. Should I have a bike fit?
168. What are single leg drills?
169. What is a turbo trainer?
170.What does feathering the brakes mean?
171. What is the basic equipment required for swimming?
172. What gear should I be in?
173. What is overgearing on a bike?
174. What gear should I leave my bike in when racked?
175. What happens if my water bottle falls out of its cage?
176. What if I puncture?
177. What intensity should I ride at on my bike?
178. What is Bonking?
179. What is Cadence?
180. What is Freewheeling?
181. What is spinning on a bike?
182. What is the difference between cycling shoes and tri shoes for the bike?
183. What position should my pedals be in when cornering?
184. What size rear cassette should I use?
185. What spare kit should I carry on my bike?
186. What tyre pressure should I run my tyres at?
187. When do I change gears?
188. When do I unclip from my pedals?
189. Will I get lost on the bike ride?
190. Will tyres make a difference on my road bike?
191. Won't I be exhausted after the bike and not be able to run?
192. What is a "Brick" session?
193. Would it help if I went to a spin class?
194. Is there anything speci!c to check for on my bike before I rack it?
195. How often should I clean my bike?
196. How do I mend a puncture?

Running

197. Do I need run speci!c running shoes or will my general trainers be ok?
198. Can I wear my running trainers on the bike to save having 2 sets of shoes?
199. Do I need elastic laces in my shoes?

200. Do I need elastic laces in my shoes?

201. How long do running shoes last before wearing out?

202. Do I need to incorporate long runs into my training if I am only competing in sprint events?

203. How can I relax more when running?

204. How do I get faster on the run?

205. How do I overcome "jelly legs" when going from bike to run?

206. How do I stop my head from bobbing up and down when running?

207. I am entering a Sprint Tri with a 5km run. How long should my long run be?

208. I am very conscience of the thud thud my feet make when running - are they supposed to sound like this?

209. I get pain across the top of my foot during and after running. What causes this?

210. I have heard that people have two pairs of running shoes - do I really need two pairs as they are very expensive?

211. I have seen running socks in my local running store. Surely these are a gimmick?

212. I love running but I am a bit of a "plodder". Would it be ok for me to try Triathlons?

213. If I feel sick because I have pushed too hard what should I do?

214. Is there an optimum time to buy running shoes?

215. My friends have suffered from black toes when running - how do I avoid this?

216. My shoulders are tense when running - how do I relax more?

217. Running shoes are complicated - how do I know if I am an overpronator, a supinator or neutral?

218. Should I go for a negative split on my runs?

219. Some people seem to take big strides and others smaller ones. Which is correct?

220. What are intervals?

221. What is a Fartlek?

222. What is a good running style?

223. What is a Tempo run?

224. What is the best way to carry a water bottle on the run?

225. What are the bene!ts of a hill session?

226. Why should I increase my running mileage slowly when I feel as though I can go a lot further?

227. What is the best way to drink water at a drinks station?

228. Do I run in the same clothes that I biked in?

Transition
229. What exactly happens at transition?
230. How many times should I check my gear in transition?
231. Do you dry yourself off after the swim?
232. Do you wear socks?
233. How can I speed up putting my socks on?
234. How do I become quicker in T1?
235. How do I become quicker in T2?
236. How do I lay my kit out in T1?.
237. How do I locate my bike?
238. Don't you get cold coming out of the pool and onto the bike?
239. I don't swim with a costume under my wetsuit - where can I get changed?
240. I have heard that some triathletes use an elastic band to tie their shoes to their bike pedals. Do I need to do this?
241. Should I leave shoes at the water's edge to put on after my swim on the way to T1?
242. The zipper on my wetsuit is stuck - can I get help?
243. What is a tidy transition?
244. Can I place a balloon on my bike to help me !nd it in T1?
245. Can friends help me in transition?

Injury
246. After I started training and after really hard sessions my quads hurt. Is this normal?
247. How do I avoid cramps?
248. How do I prevent and heal blisters?
249. How do I prevent chaffing? Can you suggest something to stop this?
250. I get sore nipples - what can I do?
251. I get a pain on the outside of my knee about 2km into my run. What is this?
252. I have heard of IT band syndrome - what is this?
253. I get a stitch - is there anything that I can do?
254. I have a head cold - can I train?
255. I have just started running and get shin splints - how can I overcome these?
256. We can say that MTSS is not exclusive to endurance athletes as I

have treated many sprinters and jumpers!

257. I seem to lose form in the later stages of my training - what can I do?

258. Is a sports bra really necessary?

259. My calves are really tight all the time - what should I do to loosen them

260. My friends seem to bounce when stretching to get a deeper effect. Is this correct?

261. My groin aches when I run - what causes this?

262. My hamstrings feel really tight - how can I loosen them?

263. My legs ache after a run - is this normal?

264. My lower back hurts after cycling - what can I do?

265. What's is lactic acid?

266. When I run my shoulders ache - can I prevent this?

267. Will I aggravate a knee injury if I swim?

Nutrition

268. How much do I need to eat during a race?

269. Are recovery drinks just a sale gimmick?

270. Do I need energy bars and gels?

271. Do I need sports drinks as well as gels or bars?

272. Do I need to take supplements?

273. How can I get instant energy if I am really struggling?

274. How close to a race can I eat?

275. What is a good pre-race breakfast?

276. How do I carry my water?

277. How much water should I drink before the race?

278. How much water should I drink during the race?

279. What are complex carbs and simple carbs and how do they affect my race?

280. What are electrolytes and do I need them?

281. What should I eat/drink after a training run or race?

282. Do I need to start carb loading for a long race and if so when?

Fitness

283. Are intervals session in all 3 disciplines really that good?

284. Do I need to take ice baths?

285. Do I need structure to my training?

286. Do I need to be consistent with my training?

287. Do I need to participate in strength training?

288. How long should I recover for before training again?
289. How many hours should I train a week?
290. How much !tness should I have before doing a triathlon?
291. How much time should I spend training on each discipline?
292. I am always stiff - how does this affect performance?
293. I am overweight - should I enter a race or wait?
294. I can only get to the gym at the weekend. Can I do weights on both days?
295. I can't train for hours each day - will I still manage to finish?
296. I feel tired after a hard day at the office - should I train?
297. I have seen lots of people in the gym doing the same weight training exercises but they all do it differently. What is the correct way?
298. I love my training and don't want to rest. Do I really have to?
299. Is it important to warm up and warm down?
300. Is it worth getting a coach?
301. Is my core strength important?
302. Is my resting heart rate important?
303. Should I develop technique before I work on speed?
304. Should I do strength training?
305. Should I go straight into lifting heavy weights at the start of my session?
306. Should I gradually ease into training?
307. Should I have a massage?
308. Should I stretch?
309. Should I take a yoga class?
310. Should I use a foam roller?
311. Should I use free weights or machines?
312. Should I taper?
313. What are heart rate training zones?
314. Which heart rate zones should I be in?
315. What exercises can I do at home or when travelling when I have a spare 15 minutes?
316. What is aerobic fitness?
317. What is anaerobic fitness?
318. What is base training?
319. What is Fartlek Training?
320. What is Lactate Threshold?
321. What is tempo pace?
322. What is the best way for a novice to get started on Tri Training?
323. What is V02 Max?

324. What sessions should I do each week?

325. What distances should I train for in each discipline every week for my race?

326. Why do I have to build up my training volume slowly?

327. What happens if I have gone too hard on the swim or bike and have no energy left at the later stages of the run?

Female

328. Can I run or race when I have my period?

329. How do I cope with hormonal changes around the time of my period?

330. How early can I start to run with a pram/stroller after giving birth?

331. How long can I run for when breast feeding?

332. What sports are best to do after having a baby?

333. I am breast feeding my baby but want to start training again and race. What should I do nutrition wise?

334. I am planning to wear a swimming costume for the swim and then put on shorts and t-shirt - do I wear a bra?

335. I have long hair and don't want to look bad in the race photos - what can I do?

336. Are there ladies only races?

337. I really feel the cold and am worried that I will not enjoy the race.

338. Should I wear underwear when racing?

339. What sports are best to do after having a baby?

340. My bike saddle is uncomfortable - what can I do?

Paratriathlon

341. What are the categories of Paratriathlon?

342. What should be my !rst point of contact to get into PT?

343. Do all races have to let me compete or can they refuse too?

344. Am I able to have assistance if needed?

345. What happens if I get a puncture on the bike and cannot repair it?

346. Are the Paratriathlon only races?

347. How old do I have to be to compete? [to be completed]

348. Is there any specialist coaching available for Paratriathletes?

349. I need a chair - how much do I need to budget for one?

Misc

350. What are the best "Golden Nuggets" of wisdom that you have learnt about Triathlon?

351. What are the most common rules that I need to be aware of?

352. Do you have a raceday checklist so I don't forget anything?

353. I would love to get my kids involved in Triathlon - what is the best way to do this?

354. Are there any pieces of non triathlon specific equipment that I should consider buying?

355. What is good running technique?

Q. No.1
What are the various distances for triathlon?

Sprint - 400m swim/20km bike/5km run (distances can vary)
Standard/Olympic – 1500m swim/40km bike/10km run
Middle Distance or 70.3 – 1900m swim/90km bike/21km run
Long Distance – 3800m swim/180km bike/42km run.

Q. No.2
Why would I train and enter a triathlon?

For yourself, for pride and a sense of achievement. You will be in better shape physically and mentally. You will feel great about yourself and your friends will be amazed. The look on people's faces when you tell them you are a triathlete can be priceless. So many people have run a 5km or 10km and found it hard. To them what you are doing is incredible.

Q. No.3
I would love to do a triathlon but It costs a lot of money - what can I do?

There is no denying that Triathlon can be an expensive sport to participate in. After all you have 3 sports to train for. When you add up the cost of entry fees, swim pool membership, good running shoes, tri specific clothing and a nice bike it can reach a considerable sum. You can minimize this though by joining a municipal pool and using your current bike or borrowing one. It will not be cheap but it will be more affordable. Look in the sales if you want to buy anything new. The end of the year is a good time especially, as companies will change the spec or color of their products for the new year. To enter a Sprint Tri you only really need swim trunks, goggles, a t-shirt, a bike of any description, a helmet and a pair of trainers. I bet that you already have most of these at home anyway so give it a go. If you like it then you can purchase more gear later.

Q. No.4
Will I come last?

The chances are that you will not, especially if you have trained for the event. The good news is that your first Tri will no doubt involve a pool swim where you give a predicted swim time. As you know you will not be fast you will start early in the proceedings and may even finish the race before the faster competitors have even started!

Q. No.5
How hard is it to do a Triathlon?

It depends if you just want to get around or go for a good time. In reality it is as hard as you want it to be. If you are unfit then it may be wise to pull out, get fit and then try again on another occasion. If you are fit then you will suffer a different hardship depending on how hard you push yourself and how much you are willing to suffer. It can very much become a mental sport as much as physical. Remember that Triathlon is an endurance sport that needs respect, by training sufficiently to complete it.

Q. No.6
What is an Age Grouper?

Everyone that is not a Pro is called an Age Grouper. This allows you to compare yourself against others of a similar age and sex and there are often prizes for each age group. You will automatically be entered into the appropriate age group when you enter a race.

Q. No.7
How am I timed?

Most races are timed by chip timing. You wear an ankle strap that contains a race chip. This is activated as soon as you start and as you pass over matting on the course. This times your swim, transitions, bike and run to give you a total time. Wear your ankle strap on your left ankle to avoid it being in contact with the chain rings on your bike.

Q. No.8
Do men and women start together?

In most races yes but there are separate starts, sometimes, in larger triathlons. Remember that in a pool based start you will all be staggered according to your predicted swim time and in mixed groups.

Q. No.9
Does everyone start at the same time?

It all depends on the race. Pool based sprint triathlons are staggered so that the slower swimmers go off first. For this very reason it is important to be realistic when stating your projected swim time on the entry form. As it is in lanes you will probably start at 30 second intervals. Open water swims will start at the same time usually with everyone already in the water. If there is an Elite field they often start first.

Q. No.10
Is there a time limit for everyone to finish?

In long distance races the time limit is usually 17 hours but it is unlikely you will be doing this for your first Tri. Most sprint or standard distance races do not have finish times unless stated in the rules. If unsure, send an email to the organizer for clarification. In pool swims slower competitors start a long time before the faster entrants so it is highly likely you will be finished and able to clap others to the finish line.

Q. No.11
Am I too old to do Triathlon?

Age is not only physical but mental. 80 year olds have completed Ironmans, but after years of training. If you are in your 60s, relatively fit and without health issues you should be able to do one with sufficient training, but seek professional medical opinion first. You will find other Age Groupers, so have people to compete against. In fact the older you are the fewer competitors, so the more chance you have of winning!

Q. No.12
Are bikes and helmets provided for a race?

No, they are not. You can ride pretty much any bike you like but it must be in roadworthy condition. That means the brakes must be working, the tyres pumped up, not squeaking or a rust bucket. Nuts and bolts must be tight. Your helmet should fit you well and not have any cracks or damage to it.

Q. No.13
Can I listen to my MP3 player?

No. This is considered dangerous and banned in most races. It takes away your concentration and you will not be able to hear any instructions marshals give or remarks from other competitors informing you they are coming past. These might be informing you that they are overtaking on a narrow section. You will also not be able to hear cars approaching, making it very dangerous.

Q. No.14
Do I need any special clothes?

Not initially apart from shorts and top, but as you develop your passion for the sport you will want to invest in specific triathlon clothing. The first item to invest in is a technical t-shirt to wick away your sweat and keep you cool. A cotton t-shirt soon becomes heavy when wet and can rub causing runner's nipple. Once you have completed a few Tri's you will soon want a tri suit and wet suit along with better running and cycling shoes. Be warned though that Triathlon is addictive and you will up your training to get better results. As a result you are likely to lose weight so buying top of the range is not wise at this stage. Wait until your weight has stabilized and then invest. We often have some great deals advertised on our website www.triathlon-questions.com so check there often.

Q. No.15
How do I find the time to train for 3 sports when I barely have enough time to train for one?

You will have to have less emphasis on one sport and spread your time over the other two. You will find that you can cut down on running as cycling will really help you with that. This also reduces the risk of injury. Swimming needs work so try to get to the pool early in the morning to fit it into your schedule. Can you run in your lunch hour? Can you run when you family have gone to bed? 20 minutes is better than nothing at all.

Q. No.16
How do I find the time to train with my home life?

This is about time management and there is no easy answer. You just have to do what you need to do and make sacrifices and compromise. For example get up an hour earlier to train, train in your lunch hour, train whilst your family are watching TV, eat dinner with your family to make up for lost time and to have quality time and conversation with them. Can you run or bike to work? Can you do core and weight training in front of the TV? Can you sit on a Turbo Trainer and watch TV with your family.

Q. No.18
Are there any Tri Clubs local to me that take beginners?

Try searching your county's triathlon association for a list of clubs near you. You are bound to find one and the vast majority are very friendly and welcoming. They should be non-elitist and welcome those new to the sport. You will often find that they hold beginners' training days, going over the basics. They will have qualified coaches to ensure your safety and help you improve. You may also like to contact your local gym such as Virgin Active to see if they have a club which you can join and train with other members.

Q. No.19
Is it worth joining my region's Triathlon governing body?

Yes. You will benefit from education and probably get reduced entry fees and insurance. The latter being very important. Consider what would happen if you hit a car or, worse, a person with no insurance. You would not drive without insurance so do not train or race without it. The cost really is minimal.

Q. No.20
Are there relay races?

Very often there are and they are a great way to get into triathlon if you only want to do one discipline.

Q. No.21
Can I still drink alcohol whilst training?

I do in moderation. I am not a pro and I have a life away from triathlon and I enjoy an occasional drink. Moderation is the key though. If you are trying to lose weight then it will not help you and only impede your progress. You have to ask yourself, if you have training the next day do you really want to be suffering and dehydrated for it? You certainly will not be at your best or get the most out of the session if you have been drinking the night before.

Q. No.22
Can I wear my surfing wetsuit?

You can, but I would not advise it. They are not designed for swimming and may even cause injury. Wetsuits designed for swimming have more maneuverability in the shoulder area and higher buoyancy in the leg area.

Q. No.23
Do I need a Heart Rate Monitor (HRM)?

Heart rate monitors are quite important to your training but not essential when you first start to train. As you progress and improve your fitness then you might wish to invest in one to gauge training zones and how hard you are working.

You can naturally gauge how hard you are working by how much you are able to speak via your PRE (Perceived Rate of Exertion). If you can only manage sporadic words then you are going too fast and working too hard. As you are just starting to build your base fitness then speed is not an issue, so if you find are unable to hold a conversation when running or cycling then walk or slow down. This is very important as you will reduce your risk of injury in addition to building the foundations of your fitness.

As you gain fitness you will be able to go longer and faster for the same effort which is when a HRM will start to become useful. Eventually you will start to incorporate hill work and speed sessions into your training and having a record of your heart rate will prove beneficial to tracking your training. Be aware that your heart rate can change naturally depending on the weather, if you have had caffeine or a number of other factors.

Q. No.24
Do I need a GPS watch?

This is very much down to budget and preference. Personally I use a Garmin 910XT which is perfect for triathlons. It is more accurate than phone based systems and also doubles up as a HRM. This particular watch will automatically record the lengths you have swum in the pool in addition to countless other features. My favourite is the virtual partner which is fantastic on race days. You set a time and it will show you if you are ahead or behind that time and by how much. It really can motivate you! The real benefit is the data that it records which helps to build a picture of what you have achieved in training and races. There is a very good interface called Garmin Connect which displays various data for you to analyse post activity.

Q. No.25
Do I need compression clothes?

Again, this is not something that you necessarily need (especially in short distance activities) but can be beneficial to reduce fatigue and even injury. It is claimed that by wearing compression clothing blood flow and oxygen to those areas are increased. The increased oxygen that is delivered to your muscles will also help to prevent lactic acid build up.

Q. No.26
Do I need padding in my shorts?

I would highly recommend this for any race over Sprint distance for your personal comfort. Most Tri suits will have padding built in and is my preferred option.

Q. No.27
Do I really have to go and train outside when it is freezing cold and blowing a gale?

This is very much dependent on what activity you are doing – you just have to dress appropriately. As long as it is not icy underfoot then it is generally safe to run. Many actively enjoy their winter runs in the elements. You may prefer to cycle indoors at the gym or on a Turbo Trainer though as the increased speed and wind chill can be uncomfortable. A lot of pro athletes will train indoors for specific sessions as a matter of course. For example on a spin bike there is no let up in your pedaling so 1 hour here may be equivalent to longer outside. You are also able to introduce structure more easily into your workouts, such as increased pace for a certain duration and repeating many sets without having to consider hills etc. It also brings many safety benefits so if in doubt or you want a specific workout, give your local gym a try. Virgin Active run numerous classes at all their gyms with many being triathlon specific.

Q. No.28
Do I really need technical sportswear or can I make do with my t-shirts?

Ideally, yes. Your regular cotton tee will soak up all your sweat making it very heavy. It may also rub and cause chaffing eventually. Technical wear will wick away moisture and keep you cooler. For proof of this, do a long run in a tee and you will see white lines all over. This is salt from your sweat. You will rarely find this on a technical tee.

Q. No.29
How do I carry my gels/bars etc?

There are a few options here. You can either wear a nutrition belt and place them inside, use a bike bag that fits on the top tube of your bike, take the lid off a cycle water bottle and put them in there in the bottle holder or simply tape them to your top tube (although I am not sure how safe this is). Your tri suit may also have pockets, which is ideal.

Q. No.30
What bars or gels should I use?

This is very much personal preference. I use Torq products as I find the bars to be moist and tasty whereas others can be very dry at the best of times let alone in a race. It recently took me 3 miles to eat one branded bar, it was so dense and dry. If you plan to only use gels and bars provided at the race (this only happens on longer races usually) then ensure that you also train with the exact same one to ensure they do not disagree with you. Never use a product or anything in a race that you have not tried and tested in training previously.

Q. No.31
How can I find out what it is like to race, without racing?

Start by entering a local 5km race just to get a feel for it – you will learn a lot, especially about pacing yourself. Most Triathlons would not happen without an army of volunteers and this is a great way to see how everything works. Speak to the organizer and say that you would like to be in the transition area where you will learn the most. In return you may get a free entry into a forthcoming race.

Q. No.32
How can I predict when I will reach the peak of my fitness?

This is very hard to do but by consulting with a fitness expert and coach you will be able to draw up a scheduled training plan that should see you reach the peak of your fitness in time for your race.

Q. No.33
How do I attach my race number to my t-shirt or expensive tri suit?

There are two ways to do this. You can either attach it with safety pins which are usually provided or use a race belt which is the preferred option. You will need to display your race number on your back during the bike section and on your front for the run. A race belt allows you to simply twist it around your waist instead of pinning numbers to your front and back.

Q. No.34
How do I stop chaffing?

There are a number of commercial products available from triathlon and running stores that are designed specifically to be applied in areas susceptible to chaffing. They use special formulas that reduce friction making things a lot more comfortable for you. Do not forget to apply such a product to the back of your neck if wearing a wetsuit.

Q. No.35
How early should I arrive at my event?

I like to arrive at least 90 minutes ahead of my start time to familiarize myself with the route, facilities and check all my gear and bike. The last thing you want is to arrive late and be flustered and panicking. Take your time, grab a coffee and have a chat with others to relax.

Q. No.36
Warming up seems like such a waste of time. Do I really have to do it?

I would recommend that you do. By completing a warm up routine you will encourage fluid to start circulating freely around your joints lubricating them ahead of exercise. Your blood will dilate meaning that oxygen can reach the muscles more readily and your muscles will be warmer and more flexible. Think of your muscles as a piece of plastic – it could be quite rigid at room temperature but if bent a few times it becomes warmer and a lot more flexible.

Q. No.37
How do I warm up?

This is really hard as the swim is the first stage of the race and you will almost certainly have cooled down a lot by the time your swim starts. I suggest getting the muscles warmed up and activated as you would before a run so at least you are a little prepared. At the pool see if there is another pool you can warm up in or even the dive pool to do some lengths and get your heart rate up.

Q. No.38
I am a bit obsessive and like to train like a demon. Is this bad?

If you over train then, yes. It is a real balancing act to get right and one that you will find out through trial and error. We seem to have a built in mechanism that tells us the more we train the better and faster we will be. This only works up to a certain point though. How you train compared to a pro is quite different. They have time and are looking for marginal gains. By training too much and not getting enough rest you are putting yourself in susceptible position to get an injury and even slow down through over training. Get at least one full day of rest per week.

Q. No.39
I am quite small and my wetsuit's arms and legs are too long. What can I do?

On most wetsuits it is fine to cut down the arms and legs which has the added benefit of making it easier to getting in and out of it. If unsure seek the advice of the shop you purchased it from.

Q. No.40
I have skipped training for a week - is it a disaster?

No, it is not. We all have work commitments or illness that can put us put for a week or two. Do not get disheartened by this as it happens to everyone and we just have to accept it. The key is to not start where you left off but at around 50-75% of your previous training volume, building up to your previous level of fitness over 2-3 weeks.

Q. No.41
I know that sleep is important but what can I do to get a better night's sleep?

Sleep really is vital for a sports person, as it is when the body repairs itself and prepares itself for the next day's training. It can often be hard to switch off, so try having a chamomile tea in the evening, reading a book and relaxing before bed.

Q. No.42
I really don't enjoy the training - what can I do?

I don't think that you should do anything in life that you do not want to do. Triathlon requires a lot of training commitment so if you do not enjoy this then it is probably best to stop and find another pastime.

Q. No.43
I want to use sun screen but when I sweat it runs into my eyes. What can I do?

This is a common problem. You are unlikely to experience this on the bike as your helmet and the wind will take the sweat away. It is a different matter on the run where this problem is most prevalent so you could try using a thicker sun screen or wear a cap or head band to soak it up and prevent it running down your face.

Q. No.44
If I am doing a lake swim, will there be lifeguards?

Lake swims will always carry a certain risk. You may cramp, be ill or even get injured. As such you will always find marshals on canoes and boats in the water to aid you if in trouble. If something does happen, then wave your arms and shout. Your wetsuit is very buoyant and will help as a flotation device. Whatever you do, don't panic. Stay calm and breath.

Q. No.45
Is it advisable to wear sunglasses even when it is overcast?

During the bike section, yes. You will at times be going quite fast and glasses offer protection from the wind (which makes your eyes water) and any debris that might otherwise hit you. Wearing them can also aid in preventing allergies.

Q. No.46
Is one thick top better than layering thinner ones for cold weather training?

You are almost always better off layering your clothes, rather than going for one thick top. Try dressing as if the temperature was 10 degrees warmer and you should be fine. If you do overheat you can always take a layer off and tie it around your waist.

Q. No.47
I am a man and really do not like the idea of wearing "tights". Do I have too?

This can be hard initially to get around mentally but it is quite normal to wear them as they are quite different from the tights ladies wear with skirts. Your knees will be protected from the wind, helping to prevent seizure and the possible onset of arthritis and your muscles will be kept warmer, resulting in a lower chance of injury.

Q. No.48
Should I have a race plan?

Yes. There is little point in just turning up and hoping for the best. If you go flat out in the swim for example it will slow you down on the bike. If you go too quickly on the bike it will slow you down on the run. As a guide, follow what you have achieved in training and add a little bit. If you average 15mph over 20 miles on a bike then it is not realistic that you will average 20mph on race day and still be able to run. Instead maybe try for 15.5 or 16mph. Once you have done a few races or if you belong to a club, you may try to stick with a fellow competitor of similar ability and then test yourself by overtaking him or her at a pre-determined point, perhaps when you know they are weaker and slower. This really brings racing alive and makes it so much more than simply racing against the clock.

Q. No.49
Should I buy my new kit at the event where there might be some good deals on?

It is great to support the businesses that have turned up to offer their services and products but unwise to use those purchases on race day unless you are familiar with them. Buy them to use in training first and then in your next race. This is especially true with footwear and nutrition. Clothing should be fine but it always pays to check.

Q. No.50
Should I go straight into a Standard distance Tri or enter a Sprint Tri first?

This will depend on your fitness levels and if you believe you can complete a Standard distance race comfortably. It may be prudent to start at a shorter distance to gain experience and then build up. By doing this you will make fewer mistakes and your training will be more gradual with less chance of injury.

Q. No.51
Should I recce the transition area and swim locations?

Absolutely. Time and time again I see triathletes lost in transition and going the wrong way. Coming out of the water it is easy to become disorientated especially as you are thinking about the race and how you will take on the bike and run leg whilst obeying all the rules. There can be a lot to think about in your first few Tri's so doing a recce is very important. Go to the pool or lake and see where the exit point is and then walk if possible to the transition area. One of the most common mistakes I have seen is people not knowing where to exit T1 with their bike and T2 when going for a run. If unsure ask a marshal who will direct you. Before eye laser surgery I even placed a pair of glasses en route so I could see where I was going a little better. You should also remember where your bike is. Try using a landmark such as a building or pylon to get your bearings.

Q. No.52
Should I take a warm top to put on after the race?

It is advisable to, yes. When running you will generate a lot of heat but when you stop that heat will start to dissipate. Your sweat will cool down and this is when you can start to feel cold. Have something old and warm that you can keep in your Tri Box to put on.

Q. No.53
Should I train on specific skills?

A good rule of thumb here is, if you think you need to then you probably do. Have a look at your times (if you have raced before) compared to others with a similar finishing time. Was there one area in which you were a lot faster or slower, including transitions? If so, take a good look at that and see how you can improve and what additional skills you need to learn or master.

Q. No.54
What do I keep my race kit in?

It all depends if the race has a "tidy" transition area or not. Most races do not - it is only larger events with competitors in their thousands that do. In this case the gear you need is kept in numbered bags in transition so nothing is kept on the ground. At most triathlons competitors will take a plastic box which they will put all their equipment into. This makes it much easier to transport your bike and equipment to registration and transition and keep it tidy when there. You can also use it to store your gear in at home so it is all in one place.

Q. No.55
What do I wear?

For your first few tris just wear what you train in and you will be fine. I wore a pair of baggy swimming shorts for the swim and then just put on a t-shirt for the bike and run which was fine. As I progressed I got a tri suit which is made of figure hugging lycra. Flapping clothes in the swim and bike are not aerodynamic and will slow you down. You may also consider a two piece tri suit if competing at longer distances as it allows you to go to the toilet a lot more easily.

Q. No.56
Should I wear underwear?

Again this is a personal decision but I choose not to, even in training. Underwear generally has seams which can rub causing friction and soreness.

Q. No.57
What training time goals should I set myself?

This so personal and all depends on your current fitness levels and how much you train. I would suggest the following initial individual targets to aim for in a Sprint Triathlon when training. You will likely be slower in the actual race as you are stringing 3 disciplines together.

To finish in a reasonable time:-
400m swim – 10 mins
25km bike – 1 hour
5km run – 30 mins

To finish in a good time:-
400m swim – 8 mins
25km bike – 54 mins
5km run – 23 mins

Q. No.58
What race time goals should I set myself?

Goals are great to have but be realistic and set them for both the short and long term. Don't over stretch yourself. Your first goal should be to finish and then worry about time in your next race. You will know personally from the training you have done how you are likely to perform. I suggest setting targets a little above your training pace so you push yourself but not too much. It is a balancing act that comes with experience. If your first race is at Olympic distance you will need to consider nutrition as you will be working for 2:30-4:00 hours which you may not have done in training. Do not go out too fast which is a classic rookie mistake. Race at your pre-determined pace and make it to the finish line. A Garmin Triathlon watch such as the 910XT is perfect for this. When you have done a couple of races you will have a better idea of where you are at and want to push yourself for a PB, remembering that at each race the weather, elevation and climate will all be different.

Q. No.59
What is the correct pace to race at?

Enter a race that is not important to you before your main event and ask yourself during it the following question:- "Am I racing at a pace that I can sustain to the finish?" The answer you want is "Maybe". If the answer is no you are going too fast and if yes then too slow. You need to balance on the edge. Try to leave all your energy on the course and discover where your limits are. If you watch a close battle between pros then you will often find them fall to the floor momentarily at the finish line. That indicates that they have got it just right and pushed themselves to the limit leaving all their energy on the course. I do not suggest that you do this though, as it must be stressful on the body.

Q. No.60
What happens at registration?

Registration can be a busy area so arrive in plenty of time. Naturally each race is different but as a guideline you will give your name and be handed a race number (if you have not already been sent one in the post) which you need to attach to your tri belt or pin to your racing top if you do not have a tri suit. You will usually be given two – one for the back of your top (cycling) and one for the front (running). They will also write your number on your arm and give you some stickers with your number on. One of these goes on your helmet and the other on your bike which is for security. You might also pick up your goody bag at this stage. You will then take your bike to T1 where the official will check it is roadworthy and that you have an undamaged helmet.

Q. No.61
What intensity should I train at?

As mentioned before in the swim, bike and run sections, this all depends on the session you are doing. As a general rule try to work to a heart rate zone that is consistent with your planned session. If you are supposed to be doing a long slow run then do that. You know that you can run faster when someone overtakes you (they might be doing a speed session for all you know) so just let them go. You have to train for yourself and not be cajoled into someone else's plan. Remember that you are building your engine which has different components that need to be worked on individually.

Q. No.62
What is a brick session?

A brick session is when you run immediately following a training bike ride to simulate the race. The bike should be quite hard and the run short totaling 20-45 minutes. This will allow your legs to become accustomed to running off the bike and help prevent jelly legs. As you near the final 200 meters of your ride start spinning the pedals to get blood into your legs. Do not engage in conversation with your family when you get home. Instead just drop your bike off, change your shoes and start your run. A gym is a great place to practise this, going from a stationary bike to the treadmill.

Q. No.63
What is periodisation?

Periodisation is a way of training to enable you to peak for a specific event. You train in a progressive fashion during a specific time frame, building up to race day. Each stage of your progression is designed to make you stronger and faster. You may do this a number of times in any one year.

Q. No.64
What is the best way to get the really sticky race number off my bike?

A good soaking usually works but don't be tempted to use any abrasive cleaning agents if it is particularly difficult. You will only end up scratching your bike.

Q. No.65
What is the best way to recover after hard training to prepare me for the next session?

As soon as you have finished, try to take a recovery drink such as Torq Recovery. This will re-stock your muscle glycogen stores using multiple-transportable carbohydrate sources combined 3:1 with whey protein. Hard training causes a strain on the body's carbohydrate stores, but also induces muscle damage and causes a breakdown of proteins within the body. With protein in your recovery drink you can not only prevent these catabolic processes from occurring, but also increase muscle repair.

Q. No.66
What is the most important aspect of training?

It is hard to point to one, but consistency in your training has to be high on the list. It takes a long time to be race fit as the transformation of your body takes a lot of work. Utilization of energy systems and cardiovascular fitness have to be built gradually which is done through consistent training, not start stop training.

Q. No.67
What is the number one rookie mistake when racing?

There are numerous mistakes but I would suggest that the most important is going off too fast and at a pace you cannot sustain. This is caused by adrenaline and being in a group of people who will "carry" you along for the first few miles. You need to run your own race and not someone else's. You find that all the people who went off quickly will slow down allowing you to overtake them later in the race. It can be hard to judge your pace so use a GPS watch such as the Garmin 910xt and make sure you are not running 7 minute miles if the fastest you have ever run is 9 min miles. The longer the race the more you will suffer.

Q. No.68
Which way around does a wetsuit suit go on?

To many outsiders this may seem a bit of a silly question but I have managed to put one on the wrong way around and inside out before… The zip should be at the back and make sure the graphics are on the outside when you put it on.

Q. No.69
Will there be enough toilets at the race for everyone to use?

Hopefully! There can huge queues though. Try to find ones that are far away as these are often the quietest. If you are a man then the long queue is often for the toilets themselves. The urinals might be free or have a short queue. I try to get up 3 hours before my race to allow my bowels to activate. This relieves anxiety at the race start and calms me down.

Q. No.70
How do I go to the toilet if I need to go?

You can either use a toilet somewhere near transition, find a bush along the route or just wee as you are cycling or running. The latter two are not easy or pleasant but if time is critical…Whatever you do, be legal and do not break any rules of the race or laws.

Q. No.71
What is a race belt?

A race belt allows you to attach your race number to it to avoid pinning it on your clothing. This means you can simply turn it around when transitioning from bike to run. I always sellotape over where I am going to punch the holes in my race number to reinforce them.

Q. No.72
What is a dismount line?

This is a line that denotes the point where you must have dismounted your bike and be on foot to run to T2.

Q. No.73
Do I need to have insurance?

You will normally have to purchase race day insurance as part of your race entry fee but please check. It usually comes included with annual membership of your governing body and is inexpensive. It should also cover you whilst training. It does not cover your bike as a rule - just personal liability. Check all policy documents carefully to determine exactly what is included.

Q. No.74
What are XTerra races?

XTerra is a brand name. Their races offer an alternative racing experience being mostly road withe cycle portion completed on mountain bikes.

Q. No.75
How do I choose a gym to join?
Visit the gyms in your area and see what they offer. Ideally you want somewhere with a pool to train in and that is open when you are

available to train. Make sure the pool is not usually closed off for kids' lessons as is often the case in mid to late afternoon. If they have a Tri club like Virgin Active then all the better!

Q. No.76
Should I drink lots of water the night before a race?

If you are doing a short distance race then just drinking recommended amounts of water should be fine. If competing in longer events and you wish to ensure you are fully hydrated then sports drinks with electrolytes are ideal as too much water can flush the salts out of your muscles.

Q. No.77
I see lots of Acronyms in fitness magazines – can you explain them please?

WU= warm up,
MS= main set
CD= cool-down
BMR = Basal Metabolic Rate
PE - Perceived Exertion
DNF - Did not Finish
DQ - Disqualified
HR - Heart Rate
HRM - Heart Rate Monitor
OLY - Olympic Distance
RICE - Rest, Ice, Compress, Elevate
TT - Time Trial

Q. No.78
What do I do with all the medals I am going to get?

Be proud of them! I like to hang all mine up so I can remember all the races that I have done. It motivates me. I prefer to get a medal rather thana t-shirt, mug or bag as these all take up space and will not be used, get worn out or broken. Medals will last forever and one day I can show them to my grandchildren, when I have them.

Q. No.79
What is the basic equipment required for swimming?

Goggle, hat, wetsuit (if required) ear plugs, de mister for your goggles, body glide, fins, hand paddles, pull buoy and a kit bag to put them all in.

Q. No.80
I am a bit ashamed of my body - can I wear a top in the swim?

Me too! You can wear a top in training but I would not bother as it will be heavy and increase drag. This can be an advantage though, to build strength. I used to place a towel outside of the pool or by the side to dry myself off and cover my embarrassing body on the way to transition. It soon encouraged me to lose weight and I have not done this for some time now. I also invested in a tri suit which covers up the wobbly bits!!

Q. No.81
What is a Masters swim session?

These are generally coached sessions and not a swim lesson and are usually for the over 25's. You will be expected to swim between 2.5-3km per hour

Q. No.82
Do I need to be able to dive for a pool swim or do you start in the water?

The only time you usually see competitors diving in is professionals and then into open water. As an amateur/age grouper you will start in the water.

Q. No.83
Do I need to be able to tumble turn or do you just touch the side and go?

You do not have to be able to tumble turn and in fact in a number of pool based races tumble turns are banned.

Q. No.84
Are you able to overtake someone in the pool if you are much faster or do you have to wait until you get to the end of that length?

Yes, you can. The form is to tap them on the foot a couple of times, when they should wait at the end of that length for you to overtake.

Q. No.85
I am not very good at swimming - is this a problem?

You will want to put in some good practice and take some lessons to improve before you start racing, iIf only to aid your confidence. Most triathletes come from running and cycling and were non swimmers or very weak so most people in the field have been where you are. Swimming is about technique mainly, so lessons are one of the best investments you can make. Brute force and fitness will only get you so far. Still, as the pool based sprints usually start according to predicted swim times (you enter this on the entry form) you will be placed with those of a similar ability.

Q. No.86
Can I swim breast stroke?

Yes, you can.

Q. No.87
Can I swim backstroke?

No you cannot for safety reasons.

Q. No.88
Do I need to be able to tumble turn or do you just touch the side and go?

You do not have to be able to tumble turn and in fact in a number of pool based races tumble turns are banned.

Q. No.89
I swim in the fast lane but there are some really slow people there - what can I do?

This is very annoying. It is best to be polite and ask what the other person is training for. That way they may get the hint and move. Or if you overtake enough they might get the message. If,of course, you are quicker than everyone in the pool then you may wish to choose to swim at another time, as you cannot really expect to have the lane to yourself. It all comes down to lane etiquette.

Q. No.90
What are swimming drills and their benefits?

Swim drills are used to develop good technique and better efficiency in the water. They are also beneficial in assisting with stroke correction. They will aid your fitness and strength allowing you to pull more water. Drills should be specific to your own stroke and needs. There is no benefit from doing drills with bad technique. Your coach should "COACH" you and not just set you drills and watch you swim up and down the pool.

Q. No.91
What happens if you touch the foot of the person in front of you and they don't let you past at the end of the length?

Try and overtake when safe to do so.

Q. No.92
I am a little scared of open water - what happens if I have a panic attack?

Turn onto your back as a wetsuit will provide buoyancy, take deep breaths and wave your arm to be rescued and look at the sky. Try to remain calm and someone will come to you very quickly to help. If concerned, then invest in a tow buoy and never swim alone when training.

Q. No.93
Do I have to wear a wetsuit?

You will be advised before the race if it is a wetsuit swim or not. Some races are borderline depending on the water temp on the day. You can hire one or buy an ex demo one for a big discount and that will be fine to start you off. The race official will be guided by the country's governing body.

Q. No.94
How can I get into my wetsuit more easily?

An old trick is to take some plastic bags to put over your feet and hand reducing friction when putting one on. I have cut down the arms and legs on mine also making them wider and therefore easier.

Q. No.95
How can I get out of my wetsuit quickly?

As you exit the water reach around and grab the leash to begin undoing the wetsuit. Then, whilst jogging to T1 take off the upper half and let it hang. Keep your goggles and swim hat on as it will be hard to pull your wetsuit over them if you are holding them. When you reach your bike push it down to your ankles and place one foot on top and pull your other leg out. Then repeat on the other side.

Q. No.96
Can I trim the legs and arms of my wetsuit?

Yes. I do this. This allows easier exit especially as I have short arms and legs. Your arm and leg should be 4 finger widths to the ankle or wrist.

Q. No.97
When do I take my wetsuit off?

Gulp some water in to the wetsuit as you are standing up at the end of the swim to aid with wetsuit removal. As soon as you exit the water unzip your wetsuit and remove the upper half. When you reach your bike pull it down over your knees and tread on it to release your legs one at a time - the "Kick and Flick"!

Q. No.98
How do I cope if the lake water is very cold?

This can be difficult as each individual is different and will have differing coping mechanisms. You can wear two caps to aid warmth on your head but you may still suffer from brain freeze when immersing your head in the cold water. By wearing ear plugs you can help to keep yourself warm by preventing water entering your inner ear. Larger goggles can help keep your face warm but you will need to demist them with a spray to prevent them fogging. Splashing your face with water will also help with the initial shock. Pee in your wetsuit. If you feel yourself getting into any difficulty or have signs of hyperthermia then stop swimming, go onto your back, raise your hand and get the attention of a marshall who will be in a boat or canoe.

Q. No.99
Should I bother to kick during my open water swim?

Absolutely YES! If you don't kick the hips and legs will drop, which causes a huge amount of drag and "uphill swimming". We need to develop a 2 or 4 beat kick in the open water to balance the stroke and prevent the hips from dropping. This also keeps the blood circulating around the legs, ready for the bike and run.

Q. No.100
How do I see where I am going in an open water swim?

This is a skill that needs to be learnt and practised. I suggest bringing your eyes just above the water every 2-8 strokes to gauge where you are and if you are on the right course. Take longer gaps, the more proficient you become. Think of yourself as a crocodile, who just raises its eyes above the water.

Q. No.101
If I get hit in the swim what should I do?

You have to take the boxer's mentality and just take it on the chin. Do not panic as it was not deliberate and just an accident. Learn from this and, if worried, next time position yourself at the back or side of the pack to avoid the washing machine effect that can be the start of an open water start. Get together with a couple of friends and practise a mass start in the safe environment of a pool.

Q. No.102
I am worried that lakes are dirty and not healthy to swim in?

The lake may appear dirty but the organiser has a duty of care to you. The water should have been tested for cleanliness and quality and the organizer should publish those results for your inspection. If in doubt, don't swim - it is only a race after all. Ensure you cover cuts and open wounds before entering the water and shower as soon as you can after your training or race. Should you feel unwell in the week after the race then consult your Doctor. The old myth of drinking a can of coke to kill off Weil's disease is not proven.

Q. No.103
Will I be able to see underwater in an open water swim?

This is dependent on the water. It is best to be prepared to have no visibility so you are ready for that circumstance. I have never swum in open water in a race where I have been able to see. ALWAYS try to swim open water before your first race, to develop confidence and open water skills. Open water coaching is available at some lakes.

Q. No.104
Will I come into contact with fish?

Unlikely as they will be scared of the noise and thrashing around! If you do, don't panic as they will be harmless.

Q. No.105
Will I be swam over?

In a mass start lake swim this is a real possibility, I am afraid. It is the nature of the sport caused by adrenaline and people trying to start quickly. The best advice if you are concerned about this is to start near the back or at the side and let the masses go and then swim in open water in a smaller group.

Q. No.106
What is drafting?

Drafting in open water can save over 30% of your energy. It is usual to draft a swimmer's hip or toes and breath to the side that the swimmer you are drafting, is positioned, also helps to save energy.

Q. No.107
What is the best way to get around a Buoy when in open water?

There are two main ways. The first one is a wide armed sweep. Imagine rowing a boat and using a wide oar stroke to turn the boat around a corner. The second uses a backstroke action to turn the buoy. For example, if you are approaching a buoy from the left, go into the buoy in front crawl and when alongside the buoy, use the arm on the outside of the buoy (left arm) to perform a single backstroke around the buoy, then flip back on to your front and settle back into front crawl.

Q. No.108
What do I do if take in a big mouthful of lake or sea water?
Spit it out, if possible.

Q. No.109
What happens if my goggles get knocked off in the swim?

Do not panic. You can try to get them back on as you go or tread water, take your time and set off again. You might feel more comfortable turning onto your back to do this before setting off again and settling into your rhythm.

Q. No.110
When do I take my goggles off after a wet suit swim?

Always take your goggles off after you have removed your wetsuit from the upper-half of your body. If you do not, then it is very hard to get the arm of your wetsuit over your hand and the goggles.

Q. No.111
What colour lenses should I have in my swim goggles?

Blue or Yellow Tint grey and cloudy days as they increase the perception of the horizon.
Smoked = Bright days to reduce glare.
Polarised = Bright days to reduce glare.

Q. No.112
How should my ankle be when swimming?

Ankles should be loose and slightly pointing inwards (your big toes should be almost brushing together in the pool). Triathletes, due to their running,usually have very stiff ankles. One way to stretch out the ligament and tendons at the front of the ankle is to sit on your heels as you would have done watching TV as a childd. Fins in the pool will also strengthen your ankles, hip flexors and leg muscles.

Q. No.113
I have a hairy chest/back/arms/legs - should I shave?

You only have to shave if you are an elite athlete or for aesthetics

Q. No.114
Should I wear a swim hat?

If it is compulsory then yes, otherwise it is a personal choice. Some consider it good hygiene to wear one (and of course shower before swimming) to help eliminate bacteria which in turn means that swimming pool operators can use less chemicals in the water. It will also help to keep your goggles in place if they are knocked during the start.

Q. No.115
Should my body be static or rotate in the swim?

Your body should rotate on the central axis. Think of yourself as a kebab on a stick being turned. The best advice is to get a good coach (not a swimming teacher as they are totally different). We are at our fastest when in our lateral rotation which is like a speed boat and not a barge. Only one shoulder should be in the water at the same time.

Q. No.116
Should my toes almost touch when kicking in the swim?

Yes, they should.

Q. No.117
What is a pull when swimming?

95% of propulsion comes from the arms and the pull is the fastest and strongest part of the propulsive phase. It is literally when a swimmer uses their forearm as a paddle to push the water behind them past the hip.

Q. No.118
What is over gliding?

We are constantly told to make our stroke length as long as possible and this is important. However, many swimmers tend to over glide. This causes a "dead spot" in the stroke when neither arm is moving. Swimmers then tend to kick hard to push through this dead spot, which wastes energy. Over gliders also tend to "put the brakes on". This is when the elbow drops in the water and the finger and hand point up towards the sky, so you are pushing against the water, rather than pulling it backwards behind you.

Q. No.119
What is bilateral breathing?

Bilateral breathing is when you take breaths on both side when swimming. This usually occurs after every 3 strokes, alternating between the right and left sides. Bilateral breathing balances the stroke and allows both arms to pull effectively. It helps to prevent repetitive injuries to the shoulder. It is also good for sighting to both sides.

Q. No.120
What is the catch when swimming?

The catch does what it says on the tin! You literally catch the water after entering the hand! The fingers should be pointed towards the bottom of the pool and you should feel the pressure of the water on your palm. The catch initiates the pull phase of the stroke.

Q. No.121
What is the recovery when swimming?

This is the only part during the stroke when the arms are not working!

This is the part when the arm is moving over the top of the water in "recovery"

Q. No.122
What shape should I be in the water?

Streamlining is the name of the game in front crawl. You need to minimise drag to increase efficiency and reduce energy expenditure. As mentioned previously the body needs to rotate on the central axis to about 40-50 degrees. Swimming flat like a barge will increase drag and frontal resistance but can cause shoulder injuries.

Q. No.123
I always really smell of chlorine after a swim session. How can I eliminate this before work?

Take a good shower and use gel (there are special anti-chlorine ones on the market for hair and body)

Q. No.124
Do I need to drink during pool training?

Yes. You would be surprised how much you sweat during a pool training session. We are using nearly every muscle in the body to stay afloat and just because we are in water, does not mean we cannot dehydrate. To prevent cramp take a bottle of fluids, like electrolytes, with you poolside and sip frequently.

Q. No.125
How do I prepare myself when nearing the end of the swim to be able to run to transition?

It is important to prepare yourself to avoid postural hypotension which occurs when all your blood goes to your legs after being horizontal in the water. Kick quickly near the end to get blood circulating efficiently ready for when you stand up and run steadily to T1. Kicking your legs vigorously also helps to warm the muscles up ready for the bike. Be careful when you exit as you may be disorientated and have wobbly legs. Take your time if needed and use the help of the marshals getting you out of the water, If it's a lake swim then it may be so ensure you get a good footing.

Q. No.126
What is a good target time to swim 400 metres?

For a triathlete 6 mins would probably place you in the top 10% and is respectable. However we know this is usually the weakest discipline for triathletes so 7-8 minutes is perfectly fine.

Q. No.127
What happens when you get out of the water – do you literally jump on the bike soaking wet?

You run to the transition area to start your bike legs whilst wet. You can of course dry yourself off but this takes time. Many athletes place a towel in T1 to stand on briefly to aid the drying of the feet.

Q. No.128
How do I get faster on the swim?

This is a book in itself but in summary:-
1. Ensure you can sight correctly if it's an open water swim. There is no point in doing a fast 600m swim when the course was only 400m!
2. Don't cross the centre line as you will snake.
3. Kick from the hips - a cycling type action can have you swimming backwards.
4. Breath from the hips
5. Pointy toes on loose legs
6. Keep your head still as it is the steering wheel of the body
7. Keep your head low in the water as a high head means the hips and legs drop causing a swimmer to swim "Up Hill"
8. For guys, don't wear baggy shorts!
9. Invest in some coached sessions to really help with your technique as an inefficient swim will affect your bike and then run.

Q. No.129
Can I ride my mountain bike?

Yes, you can and you will find many people riding them (and hybrids) in Sprint Triathlons. When I first started competing, I was regularly overtaken by guys and girls on mountain bikes who were a lot fitter than me. You will find it harder, especially if you have full suspension (lock it out if you can) as they are so much heavier and weight is everything in cycling.

Q. No.130
How can I make my mountain bike faster?

There are a few low cost things that you can do to help. The most important is to change the tyres to less knobbly versions so they roll across the road a lot faster.

Q. No.131
When should I buy a road bike?

This all depends on your budget. If you have disposable income and really enjoy cycling then by all means get one for your first race but make sure you are used to riding it. The riding position is very different and more aggressive and the handling a lot sharper. If you are on a limited budget, it makes no sense to spend hundreds or thousands of pounds on a race bike when you are entering your first few events that don't cost much to enter. As you develop your love for triathlons and move up to Standard Distance you will want a race bike, so start saving. Bike envy is a very real thing!

Q. No.132
How much should I spend on a road bike?

Around £700 will buy you a bike that you can race on happily and be competitive. Try to avoid very cheap bikes as the difference between a £300 and £700 bike is enormous. Generally, the more you spend the lighter the bike will be and the better its components. Speak to your retailer, explaining that you are doing triathlons and want a road bike that is suitable. It may be prudent to get a "sportive" bike, as these will be more comfortable, and then upgrade to something more aggressive as you progress. Perhaps the most competitive price range is £1,500. Here you will get an excellent bike that will last you for years. The rule of diminishing returns applies here as the difference between a bike at £2,000 - £5,000 is not as great as one at £750-£1,500. You will be paying for more exotic materials that are lighter, stiffer and a bike with higher end components. For most people, it is cheaper and more advisable to lose weight and get fitter than pay for lightness. We are sometimes able to offer special deals in conjunction with major retailers – please go to our website at www.triathlon-questions.com to check.

Q. No.133
Where is the best place to buy a used race bike?

Your local paper may have some advertised for sale but e-bay is probably your best option. Just be aware of shipping charges (if they will ship) and do not get carried away and over pay. For the best deals do a leaflet drop locally saying that you are looking for a race bike. You will be surprised at how many people have purchased one and only used it a few times. It has been left languishing in their garage and they have never bothered to try to sell it. You are almost doing them a favour by buying it so you can negotiate. Speak to your local bike club as the members are likely to have one or know of one for sale as they have upgraded.

Q. No.134
Isn't cycling dangerous?

Like any sport it does have its dangers so you need to think about managing them. Wear high visability clothing, use reflective strips, have good quality lights and ride sensibly. Do not ride two abreast on busy roads and do not wear headphones as you need to be able to hear traffic. This is especially true for electric cars where all you can hear is tyre noise. Make clear signals to other road users and be visible to them. Try to make eye contact with drivers at junctions to ensure you know that they know you are there. Be close to your brakes and anticipate dangers such animals in the country or cars at junctions. Be prepared to take avoidance measures. Always wear a helmet.

Q. No.135
Do I have to wear a bike helmet?
Yes. Safety is paramount and no event organizer will let you race without a helmet fit for purpose. Only fools ride without one.

Q. No.136
Do I need a bike computer?

We survived without them for decades but I believe the answer now is "yes". Depending on the number of functions and quality they can be very inexpensive and can be purchased in any bike shop. Brands to go for are Cayeye or Garmin for full sat nav abilities. Your bike computer in its most basic form will relay your current speed and distance. The more you pay the more functions you get. Popular ones include average speed, maximum speed, time, duration of ride, heart rate and cadence (if you have purchased the extra components to get these). Not only is it hugely beneficial to your training to see how far you have cycled on a training ride but also very helpful to know your average pace. If you do a regular route you will see this improve over time but do remember that conditions such as heat and wine make a huge difference to your time.

Q. No.137
Do I need a Heart Rate Monitor?
I would suggest a heart rate monitor is far more important than a bike computer. You can spend as little as £25. A HRM will allow you to train in various heart rate zones to get the maximum benefit from your training. For instance you may not wish to go over 80% of your maximum heart rate so your HRM will beep when you reach this level. It will also be indicative of your fitness. If your average heart rate was once 150 and now is 140 over the same route and at the same or quicker pace, your heart has become more efficient.

Q. No.138
Do I need a Women's specific road bike?

The geometry of a lady's bike is different to that of aman's so, ideally, yes. Ladies have a shorter torso which the frame designers take into account by having a shorter top tube, women specific saddles and narrower bars.

Q. No.139
Do I ride my bike in the same clothes that I swim in?

This is very much a personal choice but, in general, yes. Ideally, for Sprint and Standard distances you would wear a one piece tri suit. These are like a pair of cycling shorts and a vest top all in one (you would wear it under a wetsuit if wearing one for the swim). These are expensive though and you do have other options. Try to wear tight fitting swim trunks (baggy ones will slow you down due to drag in the water) and have a t-shirt[or cycling/running top ready in T1 to put on. If it is a cold day you just have to be tough and wait for the wind to dry you off. When I started out I was embarrassed about my body so I actually put a t-shirt outside the exit of the swimming pool along with a towel to dry off! If competing in a 70.3 or full Ironman then a two piece is more preferable to allow you to go to the toilet more easily.

Q. No.140
Is it ok to use a bike at the gym or a turbo trainer at home?

Absolutely. If the weather is cold and wet and you don't fancy going outside then hit the gym or turbo trainer and get an hour in there. It can be really useful as there are no down hills to coast down and you can schedule intervals into your session very easily. It is as hard or as easy as you want. The other great advantage is the ability to jump straight off the bike and onto the treadmill for a couple of miles to do a quality "Brick" session.

Q. No.141
What are clipless pedals?

Clipless pedals are like ski bindings. You clip your shoe into the pedal, attaching your shoe to it . The main systems are Shimano, Look, Time and Speedplay. It is personal preference as to which you choose and may be determined by your shoe choice. Ask in your local bike store if you can try each one out to see what is most comfortable for you as they all feel very different.

Q. No.142
Do I need clipless pedals?

Not when you are starting out, but as you progress in the sport you will want to invest in a pedal/shoe system to ensure all the power you are generating is transferred into each pedal stroke. Unlike trainers, the soles of cycling shoes are hard so do not flex, which aids the power transfe [through the whole stroke. Prices vary greatly depending on the materials used and their weight. Unless you have a top end bike there is little benefit in purchasing top of the range pedals to save a few grams.

Q. No.143
Are clipless pedals scary to use?

They certainly take getting used to but this happens very quickly. You have to remember that cycling is probably second nature and instinctive to you. You might have been riding a bike before you started school so it is ingrained into your mind that you that you can just take your foot off the pedal and put it down on the road. This is not the case with clipless pedals. You have to remember to unclip them first otherwise you will simply fall over sideways when you stop. It is something that I can almost guarantee will happen to you, as it has happened to all of us. Just brush yourself off and laugh. I strongly suggest that you practise on your driveway or somewhere away from traffic until you feel comfortable with them. If you have a Turbo Trainer, that is perfect. You will soon become accustomed to unclipping and it will become instinctive. I always unclip with my left foot (it is not necessary to unclip both when you are only stopping for a brief time) and put that foot on the floor. I do this just before a stop sign so that I am ready to place my foot down.

Q. No.144
What are Cleats?

Cleats are fitted to the soles of your cycling shoes which are then clipped into your pedals. You will find that the cleats on the side you usually take your foot out of the pedal with will need replacing more often.

Q. No.145

Are there any gears I should not use?

Yes, there are. You should not be in your biggest chainring at the front and the biggest sprocket on your cassette. This places a lot of stress on your chain, stretching it significantly, which results in it wearing out far sooner than it should. This is called cross clanging.

Q. No.146
How do I know when to change my chain and rear cassette?

The teeth on your rear sprocket will start to look like shark fins (Shimano cassettes have a tapered edge, which also looks like shark fins, which may confuse you). If you change your chain when it stretches and keep it clean, you shouldn't need to change the cassette at the same time. It's only when a chain has been stretched over a long period of time that both need changing. You can test your chain with a special tool that lays across it. Ask your local bike store for one and a demo on how to use it.

Q. No.147
Do deep rim or disk wheels make a difference?

Yes, they do. Generally deep rim wheels will cut through the air in a more aerodynamic fashion than normal wheels. They are also likely to be lighter which will aid your speed . They are expensive though, so you would be advised to invest in a good frame first and then consider your wheels. Bear in mind that they can make the handling more difficult in windy conditions, so if you are a wary rider they may not be right for you.

Q. No.148
Do I need a power meter?

Power meters are the best tool to measure performance and far outweigh measuring your heart rate/speed as a way of determining fitness. The problem is their cost which can be twice as much as a complete entry level road bike. In short, you do not need one unless you are almost pro or have very deep pockets and can decipher the results into meaningful data for you.

Q. No.149
Do I need to wear eyewear when cycling?

I recommend that you do. Eyewear will protect your eyes from the wind and any debris that may fly up and hit you. You can always use clear lenses if it is a dark and overcast day. They also help prevent dehydration and help with allergies such as dust and hay fever.

Q. No.150
Do tri bars make a huge difference?

They make a difference if you use them. The main resistance encountered on your bike is from the wind. If you are sitting up you are like one big box that is not very aerodynamic. If however you are down on the aero bars you will achieve more aero dynamics and as such will go faster for the same effort. Make sure you get in a comfortable position that you can hold for long periods. This will take some training. You do not want to come off the bike and have an aching back and shoulders. It is best to practise with aerobars as much as you can to condition yourself to them. The other main function of aerobars is to take the weight off your chest and place it on the elbows. This allows for much better breathing and stop cycling asphyxia. They also allow you to lock your body allowing you to brace against the force generated by your pedaling.

Q. No.151
Should I count the carbohydrate content in my drink within my total carbohydrate intake whilst on the bike for nutrition purposes?

Yes, you should. Your body is said to be only able to process around 90gm of carbs per hour. If the weather is hot then you should be looking to get more carbohydrates from drinks to keep you hydrated. Torq Nutrition products all contain 30gm allowing you to mix and match perfectly. So if it is cold you might have 2 bars and 1 drink or when hot 2 drinks and 1 bar. Your drink should also have electrolytes in to replenish salts.

Q. No.152
How do I get faster on the bike?

The best way to get faster is to hire a professional coach who will guide you properly and draw up an individual training plan. On a personal note I, ideally, like to ride a number of quality sessions each week comprising of one long steady ride, one tempo ride where I ride over a shorter distance but at higher speed, one interval session where I go flat out for 1-3 minutes then recover and repeat a number of times and one hill climbing session. I do all of these sessions with an adequate warm up before and a cool down after. In very general terms though – ride your bike more!

Q. No.153
How do I prepare myself when nearing the end of the bike to be able to run?

The trick here is to start spinning your pedals a little quicker to get blood flowing into your legs and activating them ready for the run.

Q. No.154
How do I push my bike to the mount line efficiently?

A common mistake is to run with your bike by holding onto the handlebars. This is very awkward as you are going to get bashed by the pedals. Instead hold the bike by the saddle and push it to the mount line. This is far more effective so practise a lot before race day.

Q. No.155
How do I rack my bike?

When you enter the bike area you will find that you have been allocated an individual number or there is a rack that is for anyone who has a race number within a certain range. Place your bike on the rack so it hangs by its saddle.

Q. No.156
Is my bike safe left on the racking?

Nothing is guaranteed but in general your bike should be very safe. You will usually be given a sticker to place on your bike and helmet (and even written on you in marker pen). Only those who are competing should be allowed into the area where your bikes are racked. To retrieve your bike you will have to show an official your race number and they will ensure it corresponds to the number on your bike.

Q. No.157
When do I take my bike off the rack?

Only take your bike off the rack when you are 100% ready to cycle and have your helmet on. If you do not have your helmet when you take your bike down you may be disqualified.

Q. No.158
How do I stop getting cold/wet feet on the bike during winter?

This is pretty hard! Try wearing neoprene over shoes, two pairs of socks with a plastic bag between. Also, if wearing Tri shoes they are likely to have a hole in the soles for water drainage. Block this with gaffer tape as road water will work its way in.

Q. No.159
How can I corner more efficiently and faster?

Again, take advice from a coach but in general pick your line, place your weight on the outer foot, lean into the corner and bend your inner knee inwards. If you start to drift, press more on the outer foot.

Q. No.160
How will I remember where I have left my bike?

You often see people searching for their bike on race day as they have got into a bit of a panic after the swim and are short of breath. I always look for a landmark to guide me to where my bike is. I also recce the swim exit and count how many rows along the racking my bike is. You could always write on your hand in a permanent marker the rough location, in case you forget. You will not be allowed to use an identifier such as balloons so please do not try.

Q. No.161
I am nervous on my bike when on the road - what can I do?
The only real way of overcoming this is to get out on the roads more and practise. Start on quieter roads and build up to busier ones. Make yourself visible and do not hug the curb. There might be debris there increasing the likelihood of a puncture. Try not to wobble and cycle in a straight line and keep your eyes ahead. The best plan of action is to

hire a coach to take you through this on safe roads and ensure that you are doing everything correctly.

Q. No.162
I am rubbish at climbing hills on a bike - what can I do?

The simply answer is to climb hills more often to get more accomplished at them. Try doing Hill Reps (refer to next question) and riding on more hilly routes. Try sitting back in your saddle and holding on to the top of your handlebars to open your chest to aid breathing. Take deep breaths before the start, to load your muscles with oxygen. Only stand up if totally necessary and try not to rock from side to side but be relaxed. The smoother you are, the better as you are wasting less energy. You could also try doing some leg squats to increase leg strength. Being lighter in your body will make a massive difference. Remember to relax as well.

Q. No.163
What are hill reps?

Hill reps are a core training session for cyclists, building strength and endurance whilst helping you to improve your climbing ability. For a Hill Rep session find a local hill that will take 4-8 minutes to climb. When you reach the top, coast back down to the bottom and do it again. Repeat up to 10 times and try to keep to the same pace throughout instead of starting quickly on the first few and then slowing down.

Q. No.164
My gears slip on my bike - are they broken?

No - they just need adjusting. I suggest that you visit a bike shop and let them do this for you or learn how to do it yourself.

Q. No.165
Should I add integrated aero bars or clip on aero bars to my road bike?

This all depends on your budget and ability. I think it is best to stick to clip on aero bars for a road bike otherwise you will have to replace all your brakes and gears as well. Clipons are great and come in all sorts of formats so pick one that is comfortable and affordable for you. The lighter and more adjustable, the more expensive, usually.

Q. No.166
Do I need Aero Bars?

If you are just starting out then no, you do not. The time to get clip on aero bars is when you are fit enough to take advantage of them and can sit in the aero position for a length of time. The biggest barrier to speed is your fitness and the wind. If you are sitting up on the bike then you act as one big drag factor. By being aerodynamic the wind can flow over you giving you more speed as you cut through the wind so they are very useful. Leaning over the front wheel somewhat does require confidence as the bike's handling abilities will be compromised. You will not be near your brake levers or gears either. If you fixed aero bars then you will find it hard to ride uphill but will fly on the flats and downhill.

Q. No.167
Should I have a bike fit?

This is a debatable issue. The cycling press state that this is the best investment that you can make, as your bike and position will be set up perfectly and uniquely for you. Coaches on the other hand tell me that it is the biggest waste of money and they have to refit all of their clients who have had one the old fashioned way with a plumb line.

Q. No.168
What are single leg drills?

Single legs drills are usually performed on a Turbo Trainer. You simply cycle with just one leg which helps develop a smooth technique and increases power in that leg.

Q. No.169
What is a turbo trainer?

A Turbo Trainer is a device that you put your rear wheel into that allows you to cycle inside. This is mainly used in the winter when it is icy or just too cold to get out. They are also used for specific fitness workouts such as intervals as they can be controlled more easily. You might also use one for one legged cycling to help increase leg strength. Some experienced cyclists from cold climates will also use them to help them prepare for extreme warm weather races. When on a Turbo you get very hot as there is no wind to cool you down, so it is ideal. At any session make sure you have a towel on the floor and on your bars to mop up the sweat you will produce. The salt within it can corrode your bike so make sure you give it a good wipe down after each session.

Q. No.170
What does feathering the brakes mean?

Feathering the brakes is lightly squeezing them to knock a small amount of speed off.

Q. No.171
What is sighting around a corner?

This is a really useful technique. Instead of looking at the Apex of the corner look around it for your exit point. You will generally go where you are looking so although you scan immediately in front of you, you should be looking a few meters ahead.

Q. No.172
What gear should I be in?

The general answer is whatever gear you feel comfortable in. Ideally, you should train yourself to get to cadence of around 100 rpm. This is however extremely aerobically taxing and takes time to develop. If you are just starting, try and maintain 90 rpm and then build up to more. The easiest thing to do is to train with other people and cycle a few gears lower, or screw the big ring down to prevent you from using it. There are two schools of thought on this. The most common believes that you should spin your pedals at a relatively high cadence (see below) so not to tax your muscles. This will allow you to go further and for longer. The other school (in a big minority) believes that you should push a harder gear and go faster.

Q. No.173
What is overgearing on a bike?

Overgearing is where you ride in a harder gear than you would usually. These sessions help develop leg strength.

Q. No.174
What gear should I leave my bike in when racked?

Leave your bike in an easy gear so it is easy to pedal when you first get onto it. You do not want a resistant gear and take forever to get momentum up.

Q. No.175
What happens if my water bottle falls out of its cage?

Always start with two bottles, not one, on any distance over 40km. You will have to make a management decision on what to do depending on how long your ride is and how far you have left. If at the beginning, then I would stop and collect it as it is vital to keep hydrated and to ensure you have consumed enough for your run as there may not be water stations on shorter courses and you do not want to be carrying a bottle around with you. I always keep a drink in T2 in case a bottle falls off near the end and I do not want to stop. It is a useful insurance policy to have. On longer races I probably would pick it up as, in the grand scheme of things, it will not cost too much time unless you are going downhill rapidly and lose it (you should not be drinking then anyway).

Q. No.176
What if I puncture?

Don't panic - it does not mean that your race is over. Stay calm and pull over to a
safe area to fix the puncture. If you are unsure about this, ask a friend who knows how to do it and practise. Practise a lot as it might happen on a training ride as well. When fixed, use the frustration it caused to your advantage and try to make up the time and benefit from the forced rest you have had.

Q. No.177
What intensity should I ride at on my bike?

This all depends on the length of your race and how fit you are. If competing in a sprint then fairly hard but leaving enough energy for the run section. Your training will determine what pace you can comfortably do. If doing a 70.3 or longer, then do not go over 85% of your maximum heart rate as this will negatively impact on your run.

Q. No.178
What is Bonking?

Bonking is when you run out of glycogen in your muscles and therefore out of energy.

Q. No.179
What is Cadence?

Cadence is how many revolutions per minute you spin the pedals. It is good to aim for 95-105 per minute, Clearly, it can be hard to count so, if you want to know, invest in a cycling computer that comes with a cadence sensor that you attach to your bike.

Q. No.180
What is Freewheeling?

Freewheeling is when you are not peddling. For example, when going downhill.

Q. No.181
What is spinning on a bike?

Spinning is where your legs turn around with little perceived effort. The idea is that your muscles are worked less, therefore you will be able to go for longer.

Q. No.182
What is the difference between cycling shoes and tri shoes for the bike?

Tri shoes usually have one Velcro strap whereas road shoes might have three, or a different system altogether. They are designed to be faster to get in and out of. You will also find that Tri specific cycling shoes might have a drainage hole in the base to allow any residual water from the swim to drain through.

Q. No.183
What position should my pedals be in when cornering?

The inner pedal (the one on the side you are leaning over on) should be upright so it does not come into contact with the road, causing you to crash.

Q. No.184
What size rear cassette should I use?

This is dependent on your ability, preference and the size of your front chainrings. I use a 12-28 which is a good all round cassette. It you have a very flat or hilly course then you may want to change this.

Q. No.185
What spare kit should I carry on my bike?

This is very much a personal decision but, at a minimum, I would suggest a pump, puncture repair kit, spare inner tube, tyre levers and money. These can all be carried in a saddle bag with the exception of your pump which can be attached to your bike.

Q. No.186
What tyre pressure should I run my tyres at?

This depends on your bike and tyre and road conditions. If you are on a road bike and it is dry than at 110 psi, but it if is wet then drop it down to 100 to give a little more grip.

Q. No.187
When do I change gears?

It is good form to change gears just before you actually need too. For example, if approaching a hill then select the gear you want to be in before you start climbing. Of course it may be a short hill which you plan to attack, in which case stay in a gear you can power up the hill in and only change down if you absolutely have too. Another indication of when to change gear is when your cranks seem to be dead at the top. They will not have any power being put through them at this stage so change to a harder gear to so there is no dead spot in your action (no power being transferred).

Q. No.188
When do I unclip from my pedals?

Ideally around 1-200 metres from the dismount line, so you are prepared for it. You may also un-velcro your shoes at this stage and rest your feet on top of your shoes. This will also save you from potentially skipping on your cleats.

Q. No.189
Will I get lost on the bike ride?

It has been known for people to go the wrong way (even pros and at championship events) but it is unlikely. If local, then try to recce the course route beforehand as it is your responsibility to know it. Most races will post a map on their website for you to analyse. During the race there will be marshals and signs directing you, so keep your eyes open for these and you should be fine. I have been in this situation when I was cycling by myself during a race and had not seen anyone or a sign for a while. Luckily I had done a recce the week before so had confidence but I did still question myself. If your course involves multiple laps then make sure you count how many you have completed.

Q. No.190
Will tyres make a difference on my road bike?

Yes, they will. Think of a high end sports car using cheap tyres. It would not grip well at all and soon be off the road. Your tyres are the one thing that connects you to the road and you might be going at 40mph downhill. You want to have faith that those tyres will not only grip very well but will also not perish under the strain. If your race is in winter then extra puncture protection is advisable, such as those found in Gators or Black Chili compound from Continental.

Q. No.191
Won't I be exhausted after the bike and not be able to run?

Not if you have done the training and have ridden the bike section at a pace you can handle. You have to respect the distance and your abilities. Also incorporate a number of brick sessions in your training so your legs become more accustomed to running off the bike.

Q. No.192
What is a "Brick" session?

A Brick session is when you do a short(ish) run immediately having finished a lengthy bike ride. This educates your muscles and gets them used to the change in motion, helping to prevent Jelly Legs.

Q. No.193
Would it help if I went to a spin class?

Some will argue that it uses slightly different muscle groups but that is probably a good thing. A spin class done at the right intensity will work you very hard and make you an all round, better cyclist. It is especially useful in the winter when it is cold and wet outside.

Q. No.194
Is there anything specific to check for on my bike before I rack it?

Tyre pressures.
That your brakes are working fully and the brake release lever (if present) is down.
Your bike computer is working
Your chain is well lubricated.
That you have end caps in place on the handlebars.

Q. No.195
What is a track or floor pump?

This is simply a pump that stands on the floor. It is larger than a hand pump and therefore inserts more air with each pump into the tyre. Most come with a pressure gauge enabling you to get the PSI you require.

Q. No.196
How often should I clean my bike?

After every ride. An old Belgian trick is to use Diesel to wash the rear cassette and chain with a paint brush and get rid of all the grime and dirt. This is far more effective than commercial cleaning products. Just remember to do it away from plants and grass and hose it down afterwards. Wash over your tyres with a sponge to get rid of any debris.

Q. No.197
How do I mend a puncture?

The first thing to remember, if mending a puncture whilst out on a ride, is to do it somewhere safe. Then follow these instructions:-
1. Place chain on smallest sproket at the rear
2. Take your wheel off.
3. Remove your tyre completely with two or three tyre levers.
4. Rub your hands around the inside of your tyre to find the object that caused the puncture. You may not find it but it is essential to check.
5. Check the outer tyre for signs of the offending object.
6. Put a little air into the inner tube and place onto the wheel rim.
7. Hook tube into the rim before hooking tyre over
8. Using your hands put the tyre back on and secure the tyre onto the rim.
9.Pump a little air in and check for pinches and bulges.
10. Place wheel back on your bike and pump fully.

Q. No.198

Do I need run specific running shoes or will my general trainers be ok?

I advise getting fitted for proper running shoes by a professional. They will talk you through the options available and put you on a treadmill to analyze your running style and make recommendations accordingly. They will look at your running "gait" to see if there is any pronation and suggest a shoe that will work with your feet to help prevent injury. It is not advisable to buy "blind" on the internet unless you know exactly which shoe you need. Shoes in last season's colours will offered at a reduced price.

Q. No.199

Can I wear my running trainers on the bike to save having 2 sets of shoes?

Many first-time triathletes will choose to ride their bike in their running shoes as it saves time and they may not yet be proficient with cycling shoes and cleats. However as you progress, you're likely to ride your bike in cycling shoes so you will need to change over at transition. The biggest advantage of cycling shoes over running shoes is their solid soles, connecting you directly to the pedals. This aids in power transfer allowing you to go faster for the same effort. Pedals are a personal choice and most road bikes will not come equipped with them as standard. This is because of differing systems that you might have already invested in. To speed up transition, try using elastic laces in your running shoes and choose a pair of cycling shoes with a quick release, Velcro strap.

Q. No.200

Do I need elastic laces in my shoes?

You do not need them but I find that they real help in races as they are faster to put on and take off. They are so much easier to use and make transition a lot faster, not having to tie laces. The other advantage is you never need to worry about the laces coming undone in the middle of your run. I recommend having at least one set of shoes for training and one for racing which have elastic laces in permanently. The reasoning behind this is that the tension can be hard to get just right with elastics so once you have it set, you do not want to have to alter it. Research, however, has shown that elastic laces do not offer as much support as traditional ones allowing for more movement which may lead to harm in the tiny muscles and tendons in your foot. You may also experience pain on the top of your foot when wearing them.

Q. No.201
How long do running shoes last before wearing out?

It is suggested that you change your shoes every 350-400 miles or 6 months but this will change depending on how heavy a runner you are. Push down on the foot bed where the ball of your foot rests, it should spring back when you remove the pressure. Also bear in mind, it may not spring back up to a day or so after a long run which is why you should rotate your footwear if you're racking up a lot of distance over a week. Some of the more minimalist lightweight shoes will wear out faster, so keep a log and if they're showing signs of wear and tear think of replacing them.

Q. No.202
Do I need to incorporate long runs into my training if I am only competing in sprint events?

Your run training should match the distance of your intended race - ie 5km for a sprint tri, 10km for a standard distance. You should aim to achieve long runs just slightly longer than your intended distance (apart from long distance tris) and complete as many of these as possible off road to make life easier on your legs and feet. By running longer distances (for example over 60 mins) you do increase the risk of injury which you have to balance with teaching the body to use fat as a source of fuel. Many triathletes find their fitness gained on long rides helps to build endurance enabling them to reduce the amount of running they do. You should make sure you increase your mileage gradually and really focus on bike fitness and doing brick sessions instead of running endless miles.

Q. No.203
How can I relax more when running?

This is a problem that I have and constantly try to work on. There are two things to consider here to enable you to be more relaxed. First of all, try to improve your general running technique, so relax your shoulders, lift your chest and keep your hands relaxed rather than clenching your fists. However, the second point is that many triathletes find they are stiff after riding their bike, so get your bike position checked out (so you're not overreaching) and make sure you relax on the bike first as this will have a knock on effect on your running form.

Q. No.204
How do I get faster on the run?

This is a book in itself and really depends on where you are currently. Generally speaking you will get faster at running by running more and running smart. Cycling will also help with your running (but not the other way around). Try to get out at least 3 times a week to run with set sessions, each with a purpose. If you do the same route at the same pace all the time then very few gains will be made speed wise after you have reached a certain level of fitness. You should try to incorporate some of the following into your runs each week, once you consider yourself to have good base fitness.

1. A long slow run and I mean slow. This is to build endurance and teach your body to burn fat for fuel. Do not go above 70% maximum heart rate. This can be incredibly hard and feel too slow but you need to do this to go faster. You may have to walk up hills
2. Intervals where you run normally and then go above race pace up for a minute or two and repeat the cycle any number of times (this is

where you get your speed from). Speed work should only account for around 6-9% of your weekly training but it is vital to getting faster.

3. Tempo sessions where you run at a pace that is just below race pace - you should be able to hold a sporadic conversation but that is it.

4. A Hill session or medium paced run.

Q. No.205
How do I overcome "jelly legs" when going from bike to run?

The first time you do a triathlon, you can feel like Bambi! But it does get better in time. Short brick sessions are the best way to get used to running off the bike. Try these at the gym, going from a treadmill to a spin bike. In a race, at the end of the bike section, try spinning the pedals more so you can hit a fast cadence when you start running.

Q. No.206
How do I stop my head from bobbing up and down when running?

This boils down to the basics of good running form and technique. Try to glide rather than bob, so your hips move forwards on a level plane rather than up and down. Good running technique comes from a strong arm action – arms bent at 90 degrees which work in an arc backwards, quick cadence and a nice heel lift which engages the hamstrings. Get a friend to watch you run or get someone to video you and see how you look! To avoid the bobbing head action, keep your eyes focused about 5ft in front of you and your chin lifted. Stay relaxed and try to enjoy your run rather than fight it.

Q. No.207
I am entering a Sprint Tri with a 5km run. How long should my long run be?

If it's your first race and you're just aiming to get round in one piece, if you can manage to build up to a continuous 5km run in training at least once, you'll be fine. A lot of fitness will come from your cycling, so try not to worry too much. Consistency with your training and little and often is more important than lengthy runs, which could wear you down and increase the risk of injury. However if you intend to be a little more competitive, then you need to think about building on your running and including speed-work and longer runs, up to 10km perhaps.

Q. No.208
I am very conscience of the thud thud my feet make when running - are they supposed to sound like this?

No. You should try to be as quiet as possible. If you are thudding you might be hitting the ground too hard. Ideally you should be looking to be as relaxed and light on your feet as possible. Try getting a running coach to ensue your gait is ok. This is a great investment in also helping to prevent injuries. I used to suffer badly from calf injuries until I had my gait looked at. I have now been injury free for the longest period ever and a lot faster!

Q. No.209
I get pain across the top of my foot during and after running. What causes this?

If you have any pain then get it looked at by a physio or sports therapist. If you wear elastic laces this may also be a cause.

Q. No.210
I have heard that people have two pairs of running shoes - do I really need two pairs as they are very expensive?

This is a good idea but an expensive one. If you run everyday and cover a fair distance then the cushioning in your shoes may become compressed. If you have two pairs you can alternate your usage and allow the resting pair to restore themselves to their proper state.

Q. No.211
I have seen running socks in my local running store. Surely these are a gimmick?

There are not a gimmick and do serve a very good purpose. Specialist Running socks provide support in the correct areas for your feet and aid in the prevention of blisters. I think it is well worth the small investment needed.

Q. No.212
I love running but I am a bit of a "plodder". Would it be ok for me to try Triathlons?

Totally. Triathlons are fun, friendly and welcoming. The greatest example of this is at the end of an Ironman during the last hour. The crowd stays on to really cheer the last contenders to the finish in what is known as Heroes Hour. You will not get this at your local race but if it is a 5km run then you know that you can walk that in 40 minutes, if needed. I used to run walk as I had not got the fitness to run all the way!

Q. No.213
If I feel sick because I have pushed too hard what should I do?

Pushing your body hard in a race or training can result in something called vascular shunt, where the blood flow is diverted to the working muscles and your digestive system can shut down. This can sometimes result in vomiting, feeling sick or diarrhoea. Pushing your body to the point where you're sick isn't to be recommended, but it can happen in races sometimes. Sometimes your choice of sports drink or gel can make you feel sick, so perhaps look at a different brand. There is no need to push yourself to the limit in any race though. You can comfortably participate in a triathlon without ever having to push yourself to that sort of level.

Q. No.214
Is there an optimum time to buy running shoes?

It is recommended to shop for a pair when your feet are warm and towards the end of the day when they're likely to be slightly bigger. You should give yourself plenty of time to try them on and make sure they feel comfortable. Test them on a treadmill if possible and always go to a specific running shop.

Q. 215
My friends have suffered from black toes when running - how do I avoid this?

This is commonly thought to be caused by ill-fitting shoes and happens to all long distance runners as one or more toes become bruised. They are unavoidable but should dissipate over time.

Q. 216
My shoulders are tense when running - how do I relax more?

I find this really hard to do as I always seem to be tense and have to be proactive in relaxing. I lift my shoulders high and then let them flop. I relax my hands and let them go loose and shake my arms.

Q. 217
Running shoes are complicated - how do I know if I am an overpronator, a supinator or neutral?

When buying new running shoes I urge you to go to a professional store where they can analyse your running gait and recommend the right shoes for you. If you have an old pair then they can be very useful to determine your style via the tread wear pattern.

Q. 218
Should I go for a negative split on my runs?

This is personal and depends on your fitness level and distance of the race. In a 5km or 10km run may find yourself doing this naturally as you are slower coming off the bike. I personally like to go for a negative split as I prefer the last half to the first. It also depends of course on the course profile. If it is downhill on the first half and uphill on the second it will be a lot harder than if on a flat course. As the distances extends it becomes increasingly more difficult to accomplish. At marathons those doing a Negative Split are generally less than 5% of the field. I'd say the key to good running in a triathlon isn't about a negative split but rather about improving your ability to run off the bike and then last the distance on tired legs

Q. 219
Some people seem to take big strides and others smaller ones. Which is correct?

This will depend on your running style. Personally I try to land and take off from my mid foot area and keep my feet under my hips. If you are taking longer strides then the chances are that you are heel striking which is effectively a braking mechanism. The idea at this stage is smaller strides but at a higher leg turnover. Elite athletes aim for 180 strides per minute to be economical and efficient.

Q. 220
What are intervals?

Interval sessions are when you work at a mixture of high and low intensity. For example after a warm up you may run 400 m at a moderate pace and then 200m very fast. You would then run 400 m at a moderate pace to recover and then 200m at a pace where your perceived exertion is 9/10 and repeating this a set number of times. Its benefits include building you cardiovascular fitness and increasing your lactate threshold enabling you to run faster for longer. These are not usually long sessions but they are very hard.

Q. 221
What is a Fartlek?

Fartlek is the Swedish word for Speedplay. It is very similar to Intervals but unstructured. A classic example would be when out for a run to pick a tree or lamppost and sprint to that, recover and then pick another object and sprint to that.

Q. 222
What is a good running style?

This is a wide reaching topic that requires a substantial answer. Instead of including one here I have included an article by Sarah Russell in Question 353.

Q. No.223
What is a Tempo run?

This is the same at a Lactate Threshold run. Essentially run for 20-45 mins at a pace around 30 seconds per mile slower than your recent 5km PB. This will teach your muscles how to use the oxygen you are taking in to aid metabolism and disperse with the lactic acid that builds up. These are great sessions for those doing longer distances. You should aim to be running at a perceived exertion of 8/10. You might like to build this up by starting at 5 mins with a 2 min recovery before repeating until you get to a point when you are more consistent and can complete 20-45 mins.

Q. No.224
What is the best way to carry a water bottle on the run?

A water bottle held in your hand will affect your arm swing and running gait, so avoid them if possible. In most races water will be provided so you won't need to carry anything. You only really need water on long runs lasting 1 hour or in very hot weather (in which case you should also be having electrolytes).Try a camelback or a special waist belt with a small bottle in it.

Q. No.225
What are the benefits of a hill session?

Hill sessions will really build your leg muscles and power output. They are hard and will take some getting used to but well worth the effort. Your body will also become more economical at running up hills. An example session might be starting with 70-90 seconds up a gentle incline x 6-8 reps and building up to 10-12 reps. Keep the pace controlled and aim to reach the same point on the hill each rep.

Q. No.226
Why should I increase my running mileage slowly when I feel as though I can go a lot further?

This is a good question and one that is hard to understand when you feel great and know you can run farther. You have to look at the big picture and the long term success you hope to achieve. All the experts suggest that you only increase your running by 10% for very good reason and that is to prevent injury. Your muscles will tone and become stronger quite quickly but your tendons and ligaments take longer to stretch and harden. If you go too far too soon it is your ligaments that are likely to cause you trouble. I suggest that you base your runs on time rather than distance. At first it will be quite natural as you are building your fitness. It is a good idea to start by adopting a run-walk plan. Run for a minute then walk for a minute and then repeat for 30 minutes. As you progress increase the running and decrease the walking until you can run for 30 minutes without walking at all. Then increase by 10% per week so 33 minutes running then 36 then 40 etc. Do not worry about your pace at all. It is all about keeping going at this stage. Build up to 1 hour runs and then you can think about building your pace and look at maybe entering a 10k race. Biomechanical imbalances are one of the biggest causes of injury, especially where the glutes[what are glutes?] are weak and the hip flexors are tight. So when increasing mileage it's also important to do strength and core work to support the body and increasing mileage. Suggest getting a biomechanical analysis done before starting to build up miles, somewhere like www.strideuk.com.

Q. No.227
What is the best way to drink water at a drinks station?

You have two options here. You may continue running and drink the water on the go, by squashing the cup to form a V at the tip which makes it a lot easier to drink from or you can stop and drink. Practise this at home before the race.

Q. No.228
Do I run in the same clothes that I biked in?

Ideally, yes. The longer you spend changing the slower your race will be. All that you change should be your shoes from cycling to running ones. Remember that you will need to wear your race number on your front during the run so if you have not invested a little in a number belt you will have to change to another pre-prepared top.

Q. No.229
What exactly happens at transition?

Transition is often referred to as the "Fourth Discipline". Being slow here can dramatically affect your time so it is well worth practising to save minutes from your over all time. The transition area is whereyou go after the swim to collect your bike and then return it again before beginning your run. Once you have been to the registration desk on the morning of the race and collected your number you will go to transition to rack your bike in a designated place. This is usually organized by race number and comprises   rows of rails that you hang your bike on by its saddle. Beside your bike you will place your gear (ideally stored in a plastic box) and lay out a towel on the floor following the advice given on PAGE X. When you have completed your swim you run to the transition area to put on your cycling helmet and shoes to begin the bike leg. From arriving at your bike to setting off should take less than 1 minute even if you have to put on socks. It is very important to secure your helmet before touching your bike otherwise you risk disqualification. Upon your return, rack your bike before taking off your helmet. Change into your running shoes and start your run leg. Remember that speed and a sense of urgency in transition is critical.

Q. No.230
How many times should I check my gear in transition?

This is a personal choice but I always get it ready, double check and then leave it alone. It can be a good idea to print a check list out of things you need to go through. I have forgotten my goggles before which is rather stupid and a list would have prevented this. Also, prepare everything the night before in case you are in a rush on race day morning. A typical list might be Goggles, swim cap, sun cream, wetsuit, run shoes, socks, number belt, drink bottle, gels and bars, bike pump, puncture repair kit, towel, plasters, bike shoes and a jacket to put on before and after the race. There is a comprehensive list at the back of this book also.

Q. No.231
Do you dry yourself off after the swim?

I did in my first transition by placing a towel outside the pool exit. I think I was the only one to do this and got some very strange looks! I would advise against it as not only will you look like a first timer, it also takes valuable time and you will dry off on the bike quickly anyway. Do take a towel to stand on to help dry your feet whilst putting your helmet on.

Q. No.232
Do you wear socks?

Some people do and others don't. Personally I do for the comfort factor. For the sake of a few seconds I think it is worth it as I will not be distracted on the bike or run by thinking about whether I am uncomfortable or not.

Q. No.233
How can I speed up putting my socks on?

The obvious answer is not to wear socks but I know that for the few seconds it takes to put them on it is worth it for the comfort. Try having them already rolled up with talc inside to allow you to easily insert your foot. Like all things, practice makes perfect.

Q. No.234
How do I become quicker in T1?
Transition is often referred to as the Fourth discipline in triathlon. It is really important to get through as quickly as you can. Even 1 minute longer than is necessary is a huge amount. On a bike that one minute probably equates to a quarter or a third of a mile! To make things quicker follow these great tips and practise them over and over again

to perfect them.

1.Have everything ready before the race and know where your bike is located.
2. Leave your helmet and glasses on your bike handles and put on before you touch your bike.
3. Have your race belt hanging off your handlebars so you can put it on quickly. Remember to attach your number first.
4. If using cycling shoes have them clipped into your pedals and held up with bands so you just have to step into them when settled on the bike.
5 Have a towel laid out if needed and have your socks half rolled up and ready to put on.
6. Have a sense of urgency.

Q. No.235
How do I become quicker in T2?

Rehydrate whilst still on your bike so you do not need to drink in transition.

Clip out of your pedals before the dismount line and run with your bike to the racking area. The most effective way to do this is by holding the bike by its saddle so the pedals are not near you.

Rack you bike before taking off your helmet.

Step into you running shoes and have elastic laces so you do not have to tie them up. (only use elastic laces if you have a specific pair of race shoes as training in them might cause injury as they do not offer the same support as conventional laces.)

Q. No.236
How do I lay my kit out in T1?

Buy a plastic box to keep all your equipment in. Place this by the side of your bike and put a towel on the ground ready to stand on to aid drying your feet. Place your helmet, glasses, gloves and number belt on your bike so they are easily accessible.

Q. No.237
How do I locate my bike?

You are not allowed to put any markers on your bike (like a balloon!) so you need to take note of its location. Look for geographical markers, such as buildings and pylons. Note how many rows back you are and how far along the row you are. You can always place a distinctive towel down to help you.

Q. No.238
Don't you get cold coming out of the pool and onto the bike?

Sometimes you will get cold but this is all part of being a triathlete – you will not always be comfortable. If you predict that you will be cold then take an extra layer to put on as it is better to be comfortable on the bike, than cold and distracted. You do this because you enjoy it so make life comfortable for yourself if time is not your main priority. There are always other races to take part in, in warmer weather. If you are seriously cold and in any doubt whether it is safe to ride or not, then stop, warm up and make an informed decision whether to carry on or not. It is only a race and not worth risking an accident on open roads. The chances of you being too cold are remote so it is not something to worry about.

Q. No.239
I don't swim with a costume under my wetsuit - where can I get changed?

Usually there are no changing facilities and even if there were they would slow you down considerably. By wearing a costume you will not break any public nudity laws or race rules. Your only option is to wear one.

Q. No.240
I have heard that some triathletes use an elastic band to tie their shoes to their bike pedals. Do I need to do this?

No, but it will aid your transition times as you become more experienced. An elastic band is looped through the rear hoop of your cycling shoe and then hooked onto your bike. This allows your shoes to sit in an upright position ready for when you go past the mount line. You then place your feet onto the top of your shoes until you have momentum and can place your feet into the shoes. The elastic bands will snap as soon as you start to pedal. This is an advanced technique that needs to be practised and confidence gained before attempting it.

Q. No.241
Should I leave shoes at the water's edge to put on after my swim on the way to T1?

No - you should be doing this barefoot unless you really cannot bear to do this.

Q. No.242
The zipper on my wetsuit is stuck - can I get help?

If this happens then I would ask a marshal for assistance in getting it undone. Do not ask a member of the public as you may be disqualified (it would be a very mean race director who did this unless you are in contention for a high placing). I would not advise asking a fellow competitor as they will naturally be racing themselves.

Q. No.243
What is a tidy transition?

Tidy transitions usually happen at longer branded races. Essentially nothing is allowed to be placed on the floor in a box. All your equipment is held in numbered bags to avoid any items being left on the floor.

Q. No.244
Can I place a balloon on my bike to help me find it in T1?

No - you cannot put anything on your bike to help you identify it.

Q. No.245

Can friends help me in transition?
You are not allowed any help from spectators in transition. If you have an issue such as your zip getting stuck then find a marshal and ask for their assistance.

Q. No.246
After I started training and after really hard sessions my quads hurt. Is this normal?

Athletes participating in running and cycling are more likely to experience muscle soreness in the quads and gastro/soleus complex. One common type of this soreness is delayed onset muscle soreness (DOMS). DOMS usually develops 24 to 48 hours post exercise and is the result of high intensity or prolonged exercise that the individual is not conditioned to tolerate. It is more prominent downhill running). Although it is a 'normal' response if your training has been planned progressively as opposed to aggressively, this should be avoided. DOMS will temporarily increase muscular tension and reduce muscle force production but can be treated with a variety of mediums including active recovery, electrotherapy, manual and soft tissue therapy, cryotherapy and flexibility work. For the most effective recovery it is wise to seek further expert help from a sports physiotherapist or alternative health professional.

Q. No.247
How do I avoid cramps?

Exercise Associated Muscle Cramping (EAMC) is an involuntary contraction of the muscle fibres causing spasm and pain. The cause of EAMC is not clear but is thought to be neuromuscular in nature and resultant from repetitive muscle contraction that increases excitatory signals. The inhibitory signal produced by passive stretching reduces the effect, which is why 'stretching out' after suffering from cramp appears to help reduce the symptoms. Each post cramp stretch should be held for 20-30 seconds.

Avoiding cramps is tricky as there is just not the evidence available yet to tell us what works. However, some methods thought to be effective are ensuring global conditioning muscular balance, including eccentric work and adequate levels of hydration and fuel (carbs and protein for tissue repair).

Q. No.248
How do I prevent and heal blisters?

Blisters are caused by compressive and shearing forces coupled with moisture to an area of skin in contact with an external force (shoes, equipment). Blisters take an average of 5 days to repair naturally with the process starting 24 hours post abrasion. Blisters are common in many sports including triathlon and can be painful and detrimental to performance. Due to the length of time for blisters to heal, prevention is obviously better than cure.

Prevention of blisters should ideally start with an assessment of your lower limb biomechanics to see if you are predisposed to blister risk. You should also ensure that all shoes you train in or equipment you use is broken in progressively and that hot spots are lubricated to help reduce the friction. Blister pads or plasters should be used to protect the skin before a blister appears. These act only as a barrier.

The fluid in blisters can be drained but it is wise to consult a health professional or medical team if at an event, to ensure reduced risk of infection. Blisters are often a pre-cursor to calluses and so good prevention and treatment of one helps the other!

Q. No.249
How do I prevent chaffing? Can you suggest something to stop this?

Chaffing is again similar to blisters but often with less force applied to the skin. This does not however mean it is any less painful. Common areas of friction excluding the feet, previously covered, are inner thigh; nipples; armpit; groin and intergluteal cleft (butt crack).

The same rules apply here as did in the blister section in ensuring all equipment is tried and tested and any areas affected by chaffing should be lubricated pre training or event by one of the various products commercially available.

The common areas listed are not exhaustive and for swim and cycling sections athletes should also consider wrist, ankle and neck chaffing from their wetsuit and saddle friction and hand blister/friction from cycling.

Q. No.250
I get sore nipples - what can I do?

Sore nipples are common in men and women athletes and most likely to occur in cold and damp conditions. The moisture is not only from weather but from perspiration and the cold from wind chill not just ambient temperature. Runner's nipple is caused by friction of an external garment on the skin area or a bra with a seam and is made worse in cold weather as the nipple is harder. Lubrication is the key preventative method here using petroleum jelly. Tthe type of clothing you use can have a bearing. For example ensure you use a seamless bra; wind proof garment when on the bike and consider what material your top is across all training sessions as some allow moisture to be 'wicked' away while others provide protection from wind and rain but are not as breathable. As with previous sections, try your equipment out!

Q. No.251
I get a pain on the outside of my knee about 2km into my run. What is this?

These questions are always tough to answer without seeing and assessing a presenting case and so could be a multitude of things. The most common type of lateral knee pain is Iliotibial Band Friction Syndrome (ITBFS), which will be covered in the next question. Other possible causes include lateral meniscus damage, patellofemoral syndrome, osteoarthritis, hamstring tendon injury, synovitis of the knee joint and common peroneal nerve injury. It is beyond the scope of this answer to detail all of these conditions but with this list one would hope it highlights the need to get an accurate diagnosis as this can determine what you should be doing with training, racing and rehabilitation. The treating therapist will want to know when and during what movement you experience pain as this can give clear indications as to the nature of your problem but is only one of many questions he/she will ask you so be clear about what you feel and when.

Q. No.252
I have heard of IT band syndrome - what is this?

Iliotibial Band Friction Syndrome (ITBFS) is an overuse injury that is common in endurance athletes including runners and cyclists and presents as lateral knee pain. The ITB is a thickened band of the fascia lata that crosses the lateral femoral condyle and attaches to both the patella and anterolateral tibia. It was long thought the pain was caused by friction of the ITB over a bursa between the lateral femoral condyle and ITB but doubt has been thrown over this theory in recent times. It is now thought that instead of a bursa a highly innervated and vascularized layer of fat and connective tissue could be the cause of pain.

Tension of ITB is affected by biomechanics and stability of the athlete around the hip region. Weakness of the hip internal and external rotator muscles can lead to poor biomechanics and increase the risk of ITBFS. This weakness is often more marked when fatigue is added to the fold and athletes will often find their symptoms become apparent at about the same time during training. The type of terrain or surface can aggravate ITBFS, with cambered and downhill training likely to be more aggravating.

Treatment needs to look at the whole kinetic chain from hip to foot and to understand what is happening during the running gait naturally (outside, not a treadmill). Initial intervention would include ice and electrotherapy with this being followed by a prolonged biomechanical correction regimen consisting of strength, flexibility and technique, soft tissue massage and tissue/myofascial release, ischaemic pressure and in extreme cases corticosteroid and surgery, although these are rare. Self-help would be to utilize foam rolling to help with mobility and fascial movement.

Q. No.253
I get a stitch - is there anything that I can do?

Stitches are another one of those ailments, the cause of which we are not sure about. There are two trains of thought: first, that an inadequate supply of blood to the vital organs due to redistribution to working muscles during exercise causes pain in the abdomen; secondly that connective tissue around the diaphragm is increasingly loaded directly after a meal if exercise is commenced to close the meal being consumed. This extra load within the abdominal area coupled with deep expiratory breathing can cause discomfort.

The obvious self help here would be to ensure you eat at least two hours before you exercise. Many athletes will leave an even longer gap than two hours but this is a very individual thing, so try different approaches in training to see what suits.

Some have suggested that you run flexed (bent over) until it subsides, however, the practicalities of this method are doubtful and will almost definitely compromise your biomechanical efficiency.
Lastly you can squeeze a hard object in your hand, a mechanism believed to help reduce pain but without a clear understanding of how it actually works.

Q. No.254
I have a head cold - can I train?

This is a tough question to answer because one must be sure that it is just a 'head cold' and that this symptom is not one presenting aspect of a wider virus that may be unfolding.

People operate effectively at set temperatures and we have natural physiological responses if we experience temperatures either above or below our normal tolerance levels, like shivering which helps to maintain our thermoneutral position. Shivering uses up our energy store relatively quickly and can reduce physical coordination thus affecting performance. A basic understanding of physical elements

will help you in being properly prepared:
- Sweat evaporation is increased in dry, windy conditions.
- Radiation is the loss of heat energy and most relevant to athletes with skin uncovered. It is more prominent in hot conditions, as in the cold the body adapts to the ambient temperature.
- Convection is the movement of air around an object/body and has implications for energy consumption and efficiency particularly for running and cycling.
- Conduction is the transfer of heat from one object to another and for triathlons relevant in water as water is 23 times more conductive than air.

To minimize heat loss the athlete must consider appropriate clothing, weather conditions, protective wear including sunscreen and energy replenishment.

Now back to the actual question!
Head colds can affect both cognitive and physical function and are reported to affect mood, alertness and well-being, reaction time, memory, information processing, speed and sleep. It is thought that exercise helps to reduce cold like symptoms depending on how severe the symptoms are. The intensity of exercise will also have a bearing as will any medication you have taken. For example, decongestants can increase the heart rate, which could make you more breathless when training with a cold. Sufferers of asthma can experience wheezing and shortness of breath and irritation of their airways. These factors can increase stress on the body and worsen any condition you have. An athlete must also consider the element of fatigue they may have with a cold and this will undoubtedly affect their efficiency.

My advice to athletes I work with is, by all means train but reduce the intensity and length of the planned session. For example, if you were planning a speed endurance session of 8 x 1000m with 2 min jog recovery but you had a cold, I would change it to a 5 or 6 mile easy to medium steady state run. If you are unable to achieve the objectives of a session planned you have to ask yourself what the point of the session is!

My parting advice on this question is if you are unsure about training especially if you are taking medication consult your GP.

Q. No.255

I have just started running and get shin splints - how can I overcome these?

Shin splints are a common term used for pain at the front of the lower leg which is generic and non-specific and covers a variety of conditions athletes may experience.

More accurately the term 'medial tibial stress syndrome (MTSS) is used to describe pain that runners often get at the front/medial border of their tibia, usually in the upper or lower third. This pain is normally quite diffuse but if it is focal, medical advice should be sought immediately to rule out a stress fracture. A pattern of pain is apparent with pain during the warm up and easing after and increased pain in the morning after training.

There are a few key points that contribute to MTSS that include poor biomechanics affecting hip, knee and foot with excessive pronation, having a strong link and correlation to MTSS.

1. Training surface and shoe
2. Fatigue as this changes biomechanics, bone mineral density (BMD)
3. Excessive or changes in training patterns have been associated with MTSS.
4. Repetitive loading and plyometrics,

Treatment choices for MTSS are rest, ice, reduction of impact training which may mean reverting to aqua based conditioning, and drills (a good chance to refine technique through drill work in the pool), foot and global biomechanics and an analysis of running gait in shoes and bare feet in the natural environment. Therapists will employ other treatments like soft tissue techniques and compression but for this condition you will need to see a sports medicine specialist/physiotherapist, as just resting will only delay another episode.

Q. No.256
I seem to lose form in the later stages of my training - what can I do?

There are two elements to this question, losing form at the end of a session and losing form towards the end of a training plan as you are nearing a race or goal.

Losing form towards the end of a session can be caused by a number of things like fatigue changing effective biomechanics which in turn can be caused by inadequate nutrition, overtraining within a session which reduces the quality of the session or a virus which at the time is asymptomatic (regular morning pulse checks can highlight illness before they appear in some cases).

Losing form toward the end of a training plan is more often due to overtraining and incorrect planning and periodisation. Remember, a training plan has to be specific to you to be most effective, particularly if you want to go on to achieve your potential.

Some key indicators that may help with recognising overtraining include disrupted sleep, high irritability, marked decrease in motivation and eagerness to train, appetite and weight changes and lower mood toward depressive state. It is thought the central nervous system influences this by changing levels of neurotransmitters (serotonin) and inflammatory mediators (cytokines).

There is no one single test but an athlete that monitors and records levels of fatigue, sleep and its quality , stress and perceived exertion may help in recognizing this syndrome before it's too late.

Question No.257
Is a sports bra really necessary?

In a word, yes!
Sports bras provide support to the breast tissue and supporting structures in both a lateral and up and downward motion. This

motion can cause trauma to Coopers Ligaments that attach the breast to the chest wall and is commonly known as 'runners breast'. Excessive motion during activities like running can cause pain but with a carefully selected sports bra this can be minimized. Key factors to consider when purchasing a sports bra should be the material it is made from, ideally of minimal stretch or elasticity, seamless cups so as not to irritate the nipple, wider shoulder straps help to distribute load and may help to negate bruising, sweat absorbent material, full figure support and bespoke fitting tailored to you as 'off the shelf' bras are made to one size and most females, as in leg length will have a slight difference from left to right which means one breast is supported more than the other one.

N.B. Women who have breast cancer can experience pain during exercise across the region of the chest band (wired) and associated oedema, which changes the fitting of the bra. If you experience this discomfort speak to your medical professional for a workable solution and consider individualized fitting. This is by no means detailed or exhaustive advice and as such individuals are advised to seek help, guidance and support from recognized organisations and medical professionals.

Q. No.258
My calves are really tight all the time - what should I do to loosen them?

Flexibility is important in ensuring you have efficient biomechanics. The obvious answer to this is to stretch your calves but the question really is how best to do this and what, if any, other treatments are out there?

Stretching post exercise should be with both straight knee and bent knee. The former will stretch gastrocnemius and the latter soleus. This is a stretch in a loaded position against a wall or immovable object, which I am sure you are familiar with. I would also consider a more passive approach albeit facilitated by sitting knees straight and flat with a towel around your feet and pulling your toes and feet towards you by pulling the towel with arms and hands. This can also

be done with knees bent as in the standing position. Proprioceptive Neuromuscular Facilitation (PNF) can also be added at this point which is commonly known as contract relax method to stretch.
You should also ensure you warm up and cool down adequately and do dynamic flexibility work after your warm up and before the main session.

More self help can come by foam rolling which should be done slowly utilising the full length of the muscle you are targeting. Foam rolling was originally devised for myofascial release work but can be effective on maintaining a degree of subtlety between soft tissue works. Caution should be taken if foam rolling for the first time as this can be uncomfortable so the density of a first roller should be considered. Soft tissue therapy includes massage and various techniques to release tension with the calves. Some of this work in this region may be painful especially if you are not used to it but it is not always necessary for the therapist to go in deep and torture you. Be confident in asking the therapist to explain what they are doing and what they are looking to effect by the technique. You should also inform the therapist what training you have done, what you intending to do over the coming days and whether you intend to compete as this will change their approach.

Q. No.259
My friends seem to bounce when stretching to get a deeper effect. Is this correct?

There are many types of stretching and all have their place. However, when selecting stretching methods one should always consider what their individual capabilities are and what they are trying to achieve. For example, you might expect a martial arts athlete or gymnast to do more ballistic stretching than, say a runner but that isn't to say that at a lower level in moderation ballistic stretching is wrong for runners. It just depends why they think they want to do it.

Bouncing or 'pulsing', the correct term, gradually desensitizes the muscle by the repeated tensing and relaxing as the body gets used to the external stimulus. Whether you need to do this as a runner is questionable as this moves from a static stretch to more dynamic in nature. This is the kind of technique we would use in rehabilitation of athletes that require greater ranges of movement at velocity at an early phase before the ballistic work later. Static stretching should be, as the name suggests, static which means to hold a position for a given period. With pulsing you are moving to dynamic which is generally done at a different time, i.e. after warm up, compared to static after cool down.

It may not be a clear cut answer but try to think of what and when you are stretching, what you want to achieve and do not just copy someone else as this regularly ends in tears as another athlete may be conditioned to this type of stretching over a long period of time.

Q. No.260
My groin aches when I run - what causes this?

This is another question that is broad and general but I will try to address the key points. The hip and groin area is a complex part of anatomy and as such is almost impossible to define in a short answer. The groin region is a combination of the abdominal structures and pelvic structures with the hip joint considered alongside these as pain can be referred from hip to groin. This anatomical region is so closely intertwined that it is impossible to make a diagnosis without assessing a patient, as many of the signs and symptoms overlap on presentation. Possible causes of groin pain can include myofascial and myofascial restriction, adductor and illiopsoas tendinopathy, pubic bone symphysis/stress, hip bursitis, abdominal wall weakness/strain or tear and possible tendinopathy and hip pain that can be caused by labral tear or chondral lesion. There are less common pathologies inclusive of apophysitis, stress fractures, nerve entrapment and lumbar spine/sacroiliac joint referred pain. There are also some medical and congenital pathologies that a health professional would consider but are beyond the scope of this answer to cover. As can be seen from the answer thus far, there are a myriad of possible causes of hip pain and so timely self or GP referral to a sports medicine specialist/physiotherapist is advised.

One aspect athletes should consider is their biomechanics, training load and how these are affected or affect fatigue. It is beneficial to have your running gait looked at when you see an expert and also have to hand your training diary.

The hip and groin region is put under a great deal of load in sport, with different stresses placed on different structures for different sports. For example, if you take part in multi directional sport you are more likely to suffer from a groin injury. However, this does not mean that as a triathlete you will not sustain an injury to this area as poor conditioning of the groin including lack of flexibility will offer muscular imbalances and restrictions in movements like breaststroke. This is an example of carefully considering what you are asking your body to do through in relation to every movement both in training and competition. If you know what you are to do, you can prepare properly for it. Makea time to think about technique work and drills post warm up.

Q. No.261
My hamstrings feel really tight - how can I loosen them?

Flexibility is important in ensuring you have efficient biomechanics. The obvious answer to this is to stretch your hamstrings but the question really is how best to do this and what, if any other treatments are out there?

Stretching post warm up should be dynamic in nature and can include high straight leg kicks to hand, arabesque (great for dynamic eccentric loading), straight leg flexion and dorsiflexion combined with toe sweep and kick outs. Dynamic flexibility work helps to prepare you for the training session ahead and, if missed, may contribute to increased tightness later on.

Static stretching post training session for hamstrings is often done by touching your toes or foot up on a wall. These methods are ok but are they stretching the hamstrings? If you watch someone touch their toes they are most probably using flexion in their back and hip to overcome hamstring restriction. The best way to avoid this is to sit on the floor with legs in front and knees straight and adopt a good upright posture. Maintain this posture as you move forward at the hip joint without flexing or curling your back. You should find that you can no longer reach your toes but that you feel the hamstring engage in a more isolated manner much earlier in the stretch. This is a true hamstring stretch as opposed to lower back.

As per your calf muscles more self help can come by way of foam rolling which should be done slowly and full length of the muscle you are targeting. Foam rolling was originally devised for myofascial release work but can be effective on maintaining a degree of subtlety between soft tissue works. Caution should be taken if foam rolling for the first time as this can be uncomfortable so the density of a first roller should be considered.

Soft tissue therapy includes massage and various techniques to release tension with the calves. Some of this work in this region may be painful especially if you are not used to it but it is not always necessary for the therapist to go in deep and torture you. Be confident in asking the therapist to explain what they are doing and what they looking to effect by the technique. You should also inform the therapist what training you have done, what you intending to do over the coming days and whether you intend to compete, as this will change their approach

Q. No.262
My legs ache after a run - is this normal?

This is not unusual and depending on the severity it may or may not be classed as DOMS, which we have already covered. General aching is fine and normal but you may find specific muscle groups ache more after specific sessions. One example of this may be when you introduce speed endurance sessions into your training and you find the calves are aching. This is often more pronounced on track training and when wearing spikes.

It is also fine to train the next day but you may need to adapt training to allow recovery or change from running or cycling on consecutive days and switch to the pool to help recovery instead. Remember that if you continue to feel aching and do not allow adequate time to recover it may lead to overtraining and that your recovery time is also your repair and adaptation time.

Q. No.263
My lower back hurts after cycling - what can I do?

There are two direct causes related to this, which are temperature, including wind, and bike set up. Other factors you should consider are the other types of training you do and if this could have affected your riding comfort. Do not assume the bike is the cause; a triathlete will put many stresses through their body so it could be something else. We have spoken about temperature in the head colds answer but on a bike the wind makes the lumbar spine area feel colder than other body parts as it can be exposed and is not a priority in terms of blood supply. Ensure you are appropriately dressed especially in cold and windy conditions.

Bike set is fairly complex to a lay person but does affect your cycling biomechanics, efficiency and power. If your seat is too high it can affect muscles groups, like hamstrings and gluteal, and place undue stress behind the knee. This improper height will make the muscles work outside their optimum range thereby reducing power, efficiency and performance. It is strongly advised to get your bike set checked at regular intervals as we do change and adapt to training, which can require subtle changes to bike set up. Experts in bike set up will look at seat height, type and position and tilt; cleat positioning and stack; crank length and shoe type as this can affect leg length. Hopefully you will have bought the correct size frame!

Question No.264
What's is lactic acid?

Lactic acid is formed from the breakdown of glucose within the body, which in turn produces adenosine triphosphate (ATP). The more glycogen and glucose (carbohydrates) you use the more lactic acid is produced. It is only during intense bouts of exercise that the levels of lactic acid are higher than what can be used fast enough. For endurance-based sports like triathlon lactate is an essential component as the levels of intensity usually ensures we can utilize all the lactic acid produced to enhance our energy supply.

In the past it was seen as the bad boy on the block as it is blamed for fatigue, cramps and muscle soreness. As you can see from the previous text, however, it is fundamental in providing adequate energy. However lactic acid does have a part to play in the reduced performance of muscles including slower reactions reduced muscular contractions and nerve and muscular conduction. This is due to the fact that lactic acid is divided by the body into a lactate ion and a hydrogen ion. The latter is the acidic part that you feel when fatigued.

Q. No.265
When I run my shoulders ache - can I prevent this?

This is a fairly common complaint and is most often related to poor running posture although as a triathlete you should ensure your swimming technique or training load is not the cause.

Many people have a 'below par' posture, which is related to lifestyle, occupation and differing ways of social interaction (mobiles, tablets and laptops). This posture adopts a more forward position of the shoulders which causes a muscular imbalance between the chest muscles (pectoralis major and minor) and muscles across the upper back. This forward position of the shoulder will undoubtedly reduce the shoulder joints' ability to externally rotate to a 'normal' range that directly impacts on the efficiency of running. If you hold your arms in a slightly internally rotated position when you run, it will lead to an increase in upper body rotation, an unwanted excessive movement that you will then have to use more energy to correct with every stride. Poor posture will also increase levels of tension that will appear to worsen with fatigue and may spread the area of discomfort to the neck. Postural awareness and correction is the method of choice for treatment and should be done with a physiotherapist who has a strong knowledge of running mechanics and corrective techniques for running biomechanics.

Q. No.266
Will I aggravate a knee injury if I swim?

Depending on what the knee injury is you may well aggravate the injury. You should seek advice from a physiotherapist as ligamentous or meniscus damage can be painful on certain strokes, especially breaststroke. If you are unsure, look at using a pull buoy or stick to front crawl or backstroke, as these are less likely to aggravate the knee joint in the same manner as breaststroke.

Q. No.267
How much do I need to eat during a race?

Unless the race is extremely long, the only nutrient you need to consider from a fuelling perspective is carbohydrate. Research suggests that the ceiling for intake of carbohydrate is 60 grams per hour, so there's no point in consuming more. In fact, if you do, it can cause stomach complaints and nausea. Combining two types of carbohydrates (Maltodextrin & Fructose) has been shown to increase carbohydrate delivery by 40%, meaning that certain formulations allow 90 grams per hour absorption. Remember that fuelling is just one part of the equation though – you also need to consider hydration.

Davids note - Torqs products have been designed to work together to provide maximum absorbtion of 90gm per hour. Each product contains 30gms so you are able to mix and match depending on your needs.

Q. No.268
Are recovery drinks just a sale gimmick?

Unfortunately in every industry there are marketing-drive companies who don't actually have a clue what they're doing, but if you find a niche recovery product from a firm you can trust, they certainly do work. The purpose of a recovery drink is primarily to re-stock glycogen (muscle carbohydrate) stores, so if your recovery drink doesn't contain much carbohydrate, it's not going to fulfil that function. It should include 1 g of carbohydrate per Kg of bodyweight. Many products fall short simply because they're not large enough. If you're 80kg and you buy a little sachet of recovery, it's just not going to have enough nutrients in it to do the job properly. Other products fall short because they focus on protein instead of carbohydrate.

Research suggest 3:1 carbohydrate:protein. The protein's primary role is to aid absorption of carbohydrate and secondary to this, it provides some material for muscular repair. Protein has a role to play, but it's not as hugely important as a lot of manufacturers will have you believe. You might find all sorts of other clever ingredients listed on the label of a recovery drink, but these are generally secondary to the roles of carbohydrate and protein, so make sure you choose one that does the correct basic job and do your research on the other nutrients.

Q. No.269
Do I need energy bars and gels?

Yes, you do, because a good energy brand will have done its homework and these 'should' be virtually fat free (because fat slows absorption dramatically) and will be a concentrated form of carbohydrate. This is better than risking a product from a supermarket that looks similar from a packaging perspective, but isn't a valid fuel source when it comes to exercise. As with the recovery drinks though, do your homework, because there are plenty of companies out there who are ready to take your money, yet bizarrely don't understand the fundamental principles of sports nutrition. For instance, look at the nutritional information on an energy bar and the fat content should be well below 5g of fat per 100g. If the bar has a chocolate or yoghurt coating, it won't work!

Davids note - make sure that the bars you choose are digestible. I have tried most and Torq is the only one in my opinion that delivers nutrition quickly but is also moist and easy to consume. Others have taken me over 25 minutes to eat they have been so dry.

Q. No.270
Do I need sports drinks as well as gels or bars?

Yes, you do, because bars and gels won't hydrate you. An energy drink will deliver energy (carbohydrate), water and electrolytes. What you need to be careful with is that you keep tabs on how much carbohydrate you're getting into your body through an energy drink and adjust your bar/gel intake accordingly. For instance, on a hot day, you may drink 1 litre of isotonic energy drink per hour to satisfy your hydration, which will also mean that you've taken on board 60 grams of carbohydrate. Therefore, you don't need any more carbohydrate through bars and gels, so don't eat them. If this continues into the next hour, still don't eat, because you're not going to gain anything from it. If you're only drinking 500ml of energy drink per hour, you're only getting 30 grams of carbohydrate, so you need to eat to make up the shortfall. So, basically, in hot weather you drink more and eat less and in cooler weather you drink less and eat more.

Davids note - Torq products allow you to consume 90gm per hour of carbohydrates.

Q. No.271
Do I need to take supplements?

There are a wide variety of supplements out there, so the most important thing to do is do your homework before you take any. Unfortunately the industry is littered with false claims, so don't believe everything you're told. We always advise that you look for a peer-reviewed published study (or studies) supporting the claims made by the manufacturer. If the claim isn't substantiated by proper research, don't believe it. Proper research doesn't mean a 'university study' it means peer-reviewed and published in a reputable journal.

Q. No.272
How can I get instant energy if I am really struggling?

A good energy product will get you out of a hole if you find yourself in it, but a good nutritional strategy should ensure that you never need a 'boost'. If you do find you need instant energy, it's likely to be because you got your fuelling strategy wrong, so consider some changes for next time. A gel when you've 'blown up' will get you home, but you won't be going very fast. When your muscle stores run out of carbohydrate, your pace drops off dramatically and there's nothing that you can take that'll raise it significantly again.

Q. No.273
How close to a race can I eat?

Preferably don't eat or drink any carbohydrate based products in the hour leading up to the race. If you have to eat, consume a very low fat energy bar or banana to keep hunger at bay.

Q. No.274
What is a good pre-race breakfast?
Beans on toast is the food of champions! Actually it's entirely up to you, but the breakfast should be low in fat. We always suggest the mantra 'eat today for tomorrow', so all of your eating should have been completed the previous day, so your carbohydrate stores should be full. Therefore there's nothing you can really do to help your performance until you start exercising, but often athletes can eat the wrong thing leading up to the race and this can have a negative impact.

If your race isn't first thing in the morning, a breakfast like beans on toast is very low in fat and high in low GI carbohydrate, so it will leave you feeling satiated and satisfied leading up to the race – meaning that you don't need to snack on anything else.

Q.No.275
How do I carry my water?

In a water bottle on your bike. Most people hydrate on the bike and do not carry a water bottle on the run. You can use any drinks stations (check if there will be any) or a special belt that holds a water bottle.

Q. No.276
How much water should I drink before the race?

I make sure I am properly hydrated the day before a race with energy drinks and water. If you have excess water you are in danger of flushing your system of much needed salts so be careful. On race day I usually have a tea or coffee when I wake up and then water or another energy drink before the race.

Q. No.277
How much water should I drink during the race?

Recent studies have shown that you only really have to drink to thirst. You will have drink stations on most races (not sprints) so find out when they are and utilise them. Remember that you can take a water bottle on your bike so make sure you hydrate before the run. Water by itself is not ideal as you are not replacing essential electrolytes which are paramount to hydration. The hotter the day the more important these are so keep hydrated.

Q. No.278
What are complex carbs and simple carbs and how do they affect my race?

Complex carbohydrates are composed of long-chain molecules whereas simple carbs are mono or disaccharides, which are singular or at most, 2 molecules joined together. Sports nutrition has moved away from the idea that complex carbohydrates are sustained delivery and simple carbs give a 'boost' – this is quite an outdated attitude. Everything now revolves around 'Glycaemic Index' or 'GI', so some simple carbs deliver energy slowly and some complex ones delivery very quickly.

Q. No.279
What are electrolytes and do I need them?

These are dissolved salts that are capable of conducting electricity, so are vital for muscle and neural (nerve) function. They also play a major role in maintaining fluid balance within the body. There are 5 electrolytes: Sodium, Chloride, Potassium, Magnesium and Calcium. The last one is less important than the other four and by far the most important are the first two. Having electrolytes in your energy drink has the following benefits:

They help to replace electrolytes lost through sweating (in case you hadn't noticed, sweat is salty). Sodium and Chloride help to maintain the volume of the blood and also help to transport nutrients into cells so that they can be used for energy production, tissue growth and repair. Potassium is present in much higher concentrations in the muscle cells than in the blood, so losses through sweating are much lower than with Sodium or Chloride. Potassium deficiency would typically be symbolised by muscle cramping. Low magnesium levels are linked to muscle fatigue and cramping too, but again losses through perspiration are less substantial than with Sodium and Chloride.

They prevent hyponatraemia. This is a rare condition that affects ultra endurance athletes and is also referred to as 'water intoxication'. If you consume water-only or an energy drink without electrolytes over a long period of time, the combination of sodium chloride loss through sweating and the dilution of the remaining salts in the blood steam with the fluid you're taking in can cause headaches, cramping, loss of strength and nausea. If left unchecked, this could become quite a serious condition.

Q. No.280
What should I eat/drink after a training run or race?

Recovery drink – as explained above, followed by normal food and a generally high carbohydrate diet.

Do I need to start carb loading for a long race and if so when?

Yes, research suggests that carbo loading will hyper-load your muscles with carbohydrate extending time to exhaustion in endurance events. The most convincing research looked at a protocol whereby 24 hours prior to the event, the subjects produced 1 X 3minute intense interval (after a good warm up of course) and then gorged on carbohydrate for the next 24 hours. This method was found to be more effective than any other in history. Some of the regimens involved a big depletion phase followed by a loading phase and it was quite uncomfortable to do, so the new method is highly practical. In the week leading up to the race, you'll be tapering your training anyway, so there need be no spectacular adjustments to diet. It's just the final 24 hours prior to competition.

Q. No.282
Are intervals session in all 3 disciplines really that good?

Yes. When you have base fitness, incorporating interval sessions into your training will bring huge gains to your performance. Your heart will be become more efficient and used to working at a higher threshold for longer, making you a lot fitter.

Q. No.283
Do I need to take ice baths?

There seems to be some debate currently as to the use of ice baths. I think the answer is to see if they work for you. The theory is that after a long or hard session it eases any swelling. As you are in ice water your blood flow will slow down but as you warm up afterwards the increased blood flow coming into your muscles will flush away waste products.

Q. No.284
Do I need structure to my training?

As someone doing shorter distances and just starting out, it is not as important as it would be if you were an elite sports person, but its always important to have a goal and a plan to achieve it.I personally cannot follow a plan, whereas I have friends who have to and we are all training for an Ironman. The best thing you can do is swim, bike and run as often as you can but try to have a purpose for each session. These might be long and slow, hill reps, intervals or a tempo run. At the end of the day if you do all three at a steady pace and can cover your race distance in each discipline then you will be fine. The other training sessions are designed not to get you around but to make you faster, stronger and more economical. I wouldn't say its not essential, I would say its maybe not as important if youre not an elite sports person, but its always important to have a goal and a plan to achieve it.

Q. No.285
Do I need to be consistent with my training?

Yes, you do. If you can only train 3 times a week then make sure you do it every week. Do not do 1 session one week and then 4 the next. You will not get the most out of your time this way. Its hard to commit but the most important thing is to not over commit and fail, start with an achievable amount of sessions i.e. 2 a week and when you have mastered this then move to 3.

Q. No.286
Do I need to participate in strength training?

Yes. This is very much an overlooked element of your training yet vitally important the longer your race The stronger you are the less prone to injury you will be and the longer you will hold correct form when racing. Your core is very important and needs proper attention - not just a few sit ups now and then. This is where a personal trainer or biometric training comes into its own. Imbalances will be able to be detected and a strength training or stretching course can be developed for you.

Q. No.287
How long should I recover for before training again?

Everyone is so different that there is no one answer. If you are fit and have been for a long time then probably not as long as someone entering their first few races. Most experienced athletes will go for a recovery run to help flush the lactic acid out of their legs and then resume normal training 2 or 3 days afterwards. If you have been on a very long run though of, say, 20 miles, it may take 4 weeks to recover fully. I strongly recommend that that you do it by feel and try not to use a race as an excuse not to train for days or weeks on end.

Q. No.288
How many hours should I train a week?

This all depends on what length of Triathlon you are doing and how well you wish to do. As a guide you could get around a Sprint having only done minimal training in a gym of maybe 3 hours a week but to be a little more competitive you would need to be doing at least 3-8 hours. At Olympic distance you could get away with 5 hours but really 5-10 hours would be ideal. For 70.3 and Ironman then 10-20 hours a week is more realistic. Pros will train for between 25 and 35 hours a week from Olympic to Ironman to give you an idea. There is evidence that the gains from training for over 3 hours are very minimal and should be reserved for those going for the win. The exception to this is for those training for an Ironman, as 4-6 hour bike rides need to be part of your endurance training.

Q. No.289
How much fitness should I have before doing a triathlon?

You need a moderate amount of fitness to enjoy doing even a sprint. As a guide and to be comfortable you should be able to run a stand alone 5km in under 30 mins and bike 10 miles in under 40.

Q. No.290
How much time should I spend training on each discipline?

Cycling is the longest discipline so it makes sense to train more in that. Next prioritise running, then swimming. Out of the three swimming is the most technical so spending time getting that right is hugely important. You can exert too much effort into you swim by poor technique that it can severely affect your bike performance.

Q. No.291
I am always stiff - how does this affect performance?

This is a result of pushing yourself and using new muscle groups or not recovering well enough. Try stretching more, eating healthy, nutrient rich food and getting enough rest and sleep.

Q. No.292
I am overweight - should I enter a race or wait?

You need to see your Doctor and get clearance that it is safe to race and will not be too much of a strain on your heart. If you do not feel fit enough then wait for another day. Even a Sprint Tri can take almost 110 minutes which is hard on your body and heart. I have competed when overweight and not very fit and finished in the bottom 10%. I now use this as inspiration and hope to finish the same race in the top 20% each year.

Q. No.293
I can only get to the gym at the weekend. Can I do weights on both days?

You should not train the same muscle group twice within 24 hours. The muscles need 48 hours to rest which is when they grow and become stronger. If you train our lower body on a Saturday then work on your upper on Sunday. Can you get a mat and some weights for home for a 30 minute session if you cannot get to the gym during the week?

Q. No.294
I can't train for hours each day - will I still manage to finish?

This all depends on the distance. You will be able to finish a sprint on relatively little training but an Olympic distance event does take commitment. You will be racing for 2:30 -3:30 hours probably in your first one (unless you are very fit anyway) so should be able to train for that length of time continuously at least once or be very close to it. The more you train and the smarter you train the faster you will be.

Question No.295
I feel tired after a hard day at the office - should I train?

Often you are mentally tired and not physically tired. Lots of people find that going for a run beats the stress out of them and they feel great after a run and often post a PB on their regular course. If you are likely to come home and have a bottle of wine as you have been stressed then opting for a run instead is a double win. Not only will you save all those empty calories you will be burning them, so a double benefit.

Question No.296
I have seen lots of people in the gym doing the same weight training exercises but they all do it differently. What is the correct way?

There are different grips that people use on what appears to be the same exercise. By changing the grip they might be using a different muscle or working one in a different way. They could of course be doing it all wrong! Your best bet is to find an experienced trainer who can guide you through what you need to do.

Question No.297
I love my training and don't want to rest. Do I really have to?

Totally. Rest is mandatory to help your body recover from the vigours of training and repair itself. If you choose not to rest then you increase risk of illness, burnout, over-training and injury. Just because your friend has boasted on Facebook that they have just smashed a 60 mile ride it does not mean that you have to. Follow your plan and stick to it and listen to your body.

Question No.298
Is it important to warm up and warm down?

It is yes and it applies to both training and race day. It can often be hard on race day with the swim first so just go for a light jog to get the blood flowing around your body.

Question No.299
Is it worth getting a coach?

If you are serious and can afford one, then yes. All the pros have one and they know what they are doing. A good coach knows how to train you, can see your weak and strong points and work on them. They can often spot that you are not feeling 100% and tell you to ease off. They will be able to see potential injuries before they happen due to your biometrics and help you prevent them by giving you relevant strength training to do. They will ensure that as long as you put the work in you will perform to the best of your ability.

Question No.300
Is my core strength important?

It is very important. Your core holds you together and helps keep good form especially at the later stages of a race. You need a proper program and not just a few sit ups here and there. I really cannot stress how important having good core strength is.

Q. No.301
Is my resting heart rate important?

A low resting heart rate is an indicator of your hearts ability to pump blood around your body efficiently. It will come down as you are fitter. You can also use it as a reliable indicator to forthcoming illness. If you know your resting rate and feel under the weather one morning take another reading. If it is higher than normal take a rest day. It is all about listening to your body.

Q. No.302
Should I develop technique before I work on speed?

Absolutely. Ability will only get you so far before you plateau. By having good technique you can train for longer and faster without such a high risk of injury. This is highlighted in swimming where technique is everything. You may find that you have to go slower to correct your technique before you can go faster.

Q. No.303
Should I do strength training?

There are many schools of thought on this. I say yes but focus on your core and toning your arms and shoulders. Your arms and legs will get a good workout anyway from your swim, bike and run.

Q. No.304
Should I go straight into lifting heavy weights at the start of my session?

No - you do not want to lift heavy weights and build bulk anyway. Your objective should be to tone and strengthen only. Start by using a light weight initially to wake up your muscles and get blood pumping through them as a warm up before doing your main sets. You only need to do this for the first time you work a muscle group within each session.

Q. No.305
Should I gradually ease into training?

Yes this is advisable. You do not want to suddenly stress your body and be plagued by injury. This is surprisingly easy to do, so be careful especially with running. Your speed and the distance you can run will seem to increase quite quickly but your muscles, tendons and ligaments will not grow and strengthen at such a fast pace. The latter two, in particular, need to be built up slowly so the rule is only to increase mileage by around 10% per week. You will be limited naturally by what you can do physically at first so build up to being able to jog for 30 mins without walking and then increase your time by 3 mins the next week and so on. After 4 weeks when you are at 40 miles increase in 4 minute sections per run.

Q. No.306
Should I have a massage?

I believe so but do not rely on them. I suggest having one per week if you can afford it. The rest of the time focus on self-massage and using foam rollers, having taken professional advice on how to use them correctly.

Q. No.307
Should I stretch?

There are many different views on how and when it is most beneficial to stretch. I suggest you undertake further reading on the subject to gain a better understand the various and current views. Then take advice from a professional to design a stretching plan that is consistent with your need and to enable you to perform stretches with the correct form.

Q. No.308
Should I take a yoga class?

I believe that yoga is of great benefit to triathletes, so would suggest it.

Q. No.309
Should I use a foam roller?

Yes. Self-massage and using items like a foam roller are essential to keep injuries at bay and to aid your recovery. Read the instructions carefully and consult a fitness professional if unsure how to use these properly.

Q. No.310
Should I use free weights or machines?

Both have their place. Free weights are fantastic as you are in total control and take all the load. You will utilize your core muscles more as you have to balance and it can help to create balance in your body. Machine weights control the range of motion that you will go through and will bear some of the weight. They are safer as it is a lot harder to fall over or do the exercise incorrectly. Using a combination of both is the most logical approach.

Q. No.311
Should I Taper?

It all depends on how long your race is. If doing a sprint then you may not need one at all but it is not advisable to do any long or hard sessions the day before. If doing an Ironman you may have a 3 week taper where you reduce your training levels down leaving you in peak condition on race day. It can be hard to determine when you need to start so it is good to have a race or two before your "A" race of the season to test yourself.

Q. No.312
What are heart rate training zones?

Heart rate training zones correspond to a percentage of your maximum heart rate that you are training at. The purpose being to train in specific zones for different gains. Zones are usually broken down into 5 or 6 zones but determining what those zones are for you personally is very hard. For example, your heart rate may vary depending on a number of different factors such as the temperature or if you have had coffee etc. Therefore it is regarded as not the most accurate way to train but still effective. To gain the most from training by heart rate I suggest that you have your zones determined by a professional for personal accuracy.

Q. No.313
Which heart rate zones should I be in?

This all depends what you are trying to achieve over all and in each individual session. For example, to build aerobic fitness you will want to be in Zone 2 for most of your workouts. This may feel incredibly slow but stick with it. You may even have to walk up hills to keep your heart rate down sufficiently.

Q. No.314
What exercises can I do at home or when travelling when I have a spare 15 minutes?

There is a lot you can do but the most obvious are stair climbing, push ups, squats, crunches, planks or skipping. The TRX system of training is ideal to do at home if you short of time.. Also consider self massage with a foam roller. This can even be done whilst watching the TV!

Q. No.315
What is aerobic fitness?

Aerobic fitness is your ability to sustain an activity for a prolonged length of time. When training aerobically your body uses oxygen which is circulated through your system via your lungs and blood to provide energy. The more trained you are the more oxygen your body can use. You can test this by having a V02 max test.

Q. No.316
What is anaerobic fitness?

Anaerobic fitness is where the body uses fuel stored in your body to power it. You can only sustain this for a short amount of time before depleting your reserves. A sprinter for example would be working anaerobically whilst a mid-distance athlete might be using a mixture of anaerobic and aerobic fuel systems.

Q. No.317
What is base training?

Base training is building up your "base" fitness. This acts as your backbone and allows you to then do more focused training such as fartlek hill repeats, tempo work and race pace sessions for example. Think of it as your foundation fitness that allows you to train hard after completion. If you have been off injured then you cannot come back straight where you left off, but if you have some base fitness still you will be in better stead.

Q. No.318
What is Fartlek Training?

Fartlek is a Swedish term that translates into "Speedplay". For example you decide to sprint to the next lamp post, recover and then do the same multiple times throughout your run.

Question No.319
What is Lactate Threshold?

Lactate Threshold is the point at which lactic acid accumulates in your blood stream. This is something that you can test for and is highly useful for your training if competing in longer events. By knowing when your body starts to produce it you can train under that threshold and keep going for longer. I have for example have had a routine test done by Torq Fitness to determine my lactate threshold. This works out when lactic acid was being produced by my body by using a power meter whilst on a Turbo Trainer. Every 5 minutes I increased the Watts I was cycling at whilst my coach took a blood sample (which you do not feel) for analysis in a special machine much like a diabetic would test their blood sugar levels with. This determined the point at which my body produced lactic acid and my corresponding heart rate. As mentioned previously, your heart rate can be variable but this provides a far more exact set of figures than one purely designed around maximum heart rate. I now know what I need to keep my heart rate under to avoid lactic acid production which is essential knowledge for long distance races.

Question No.320
What is tempo pace?

Tempo runs are completed after a warm up and generally last for around 15-50 minutes before cooling down. Your run should feel comfortably hard and be just below your 10km race pace. These runs will teach your body to be more efficient meaning you will tire less quickly and increase your lactate threshold.

Q. No.321
What is the best way for a novice to get started on Tri Training?

The first step is to get out of your home and go running, cycling and swimming. Take it easy to start with and build up slowly. If you have no real fitness then start out on the bike to build some cardio fitness before you start jogging. When you feel ready to jog then it is fine to jog for a while and then have a recovery walk before jogging again. You need to build up the time you spend doing these activities rather than distance. You can start swimming when you like and try to get 2-3 sessions in per week.

Q. No.322
What is V02 Max?

Vo2 Max is the maximum amount of oxygen your body can use during exercise. The higher the number, the fitter you are. To discover what yours is you will need to perform a controlled test with a professional. Typically this will involve you being on a treadmill and the speed or incline increased to make you work harder until you can go no further. You will have a mask strapped to your face that is connected to a computer which provides the analysis.

Q. No.323
What sessions should I do each week?

This is very much personal but I would suggest one each of the following for each discipline as a minimum:-
1. A long steady session.
2. Intervals.
3. Tempo.

Q. No.324
What distances should I train for in each discipline every week for my race?

As a general rule of thumb I suggest that you cover 3 times the race distance over the course of each week for a Sprint Tri. For example, if the race ends in a 5km run then run 15km in total each week once you have worked up to it. This should really be a minimum to allow you to put in a half decent performance. If you just want to finish then you might reduce it to 2 times with each "long" session being equal to your race distance. Every 4th week reduce the mileage and have a rest week allowing your body to recover. Reduce by 50-70% as a guide.

Q. No.325
Why do I have to build up my training volume slowly?

To avoid injury. This is especially true with running. Your muscles and fitness will strengthen and increase relatively quickly giving you a lot of confidence to run faster and for longer. The problem is that your tendons and ligaments harden up a lot slower so an imbalance occurs causing injury. It is best to increase at a rate of 10% per week from s base of 30 minutes running. Rest is also important and initially I advise running every other day to allow your body to grow and adapt.

Q. No.326
What happens if I have gone too hard on the swim or bike and have no energy left at the later stages of the run?

Then you have learnt a good lesson in pacing yourself to complete the whole race. It is hard but you will have learnt a lot.It may be that you are pushing yourself to the limit causing fatigue or it may be because of the conditions. If you have always trained in moderate conditions and it is hot on race day you will have to make allowances for that. Similarly if you have trained on flat lands and the race is hilly you could suffer badly. It is good to push hard and find where your limits are but try and do this in races that are not important. If you find you have no energy left then seek sugar. Coke is said to do wonders to give you an instant hit or try carrying gels (these take 15 mins or so to work). They say that pushing your swim time by 2 minutes can cost you 20 minutes on the bike in an Ironman so be careful to swim hard but do not go aerobic. The same goes for the bike. Do not go over 85% of your maximum heart rate on an Ironman or you will suffer on the run.

Q. No.327
Can I run or race when I have my period?

Yes - take extra supplies with you. But be careful if you feel nauseous. It may be advisable to consult your Doctor or nutritionist regarding any supplements such as Iron and B Vitamins that you might require to enable you to undertake endurance work.

Q. No.328
How do I cope with hormonal changes around the time of my period?

Exercise is one of the best forms of stress relief prior to menstruating. You may feel more tired or lethargic but there is no problem with exercise at this time. You may not feel like it but the fresh air can do wonders for you.

Q. No.329
How early can I start to run with a pram/stroller after giving birth?

There are mixed views on this but consult your Doctor after your 6 week check to ensure that they think it is ok for your to start training. If you are a trained athlete and have previous children then you may be able to start sooner but seek professional medical opinion.

Q. No.330
How long can I run for when breast feeding?

This is very personal and depends how often you need to express milk to avoid your breasts getting swollen and uncomfortable. You will gauge through experience.

Q. No.331
What sports are best to do after having a baby?

Swimming is probably the best as it is non weight bearing complemented by Pilates and yogo which will strengthen your core muscles to give you a solid body to start training and help avoid injury.

Q. No.332
I am breast feeding my baby but want to start training again and race. What should I do nutrition wise?

As long as you are fuelling your runs sufficiently you should be fine. Your diet should contain a good amount of fruit and vegetables from all colour groups. Consult a nutritionist regarding the safety of using gels etc. Swimming is a good way to start training again as you will generally be doing it for less time than running or cycling.

Q. No.333
I am planning to wear a swimming costume for the swim and then put on shorts and t-shirt - do I wear a bra?

This is optional but you can wear a sports bra under your costume to offer support when running and cycling. Some swimming costumes have built in support or you can invest in a tri suit.

Q. No.334
I have long hair and don't want to look bad in the race photos - what can I do?

Having it in a Pony Tail will help or having it a little shorter if it is that much of a concern. Remember that you will also be wearing a bike helmet and you want a properly fitting helmet. You do not want grips as these may pierce your swim cap if wearing one.

Q. No.335
Are there ladies only races?

Yes, there are. Bigger mixed sex races often have ladies only changing tents which you can change in. Most triathlons do not offer any changing area in the transition zone.

Q. No.336
I really feel the cold and am worried that I will not enjoy the race.

This is quite common for males and females. All you can do is dress appropriately but think of how warm you will get on the cycle and run.

Q. No.337
Should I wear underwear when racing?

No. Underwear will not dry as quickly as your tri suit and could cause irritation. Also it will have seams which could cause chafing. The only exception is a sports bra.

Q. No.338
What sports are best to do after having a baby?

Swimming is probably the best as it is non weight bearing complemented by Pilates and yogo which will strengthen your core muscles to give you a solid body to start training and help avoid injury.

Q. No.339
My bike saddle is uncomfortable - what can I do?

There are many options when it comes to saddles and it is important to get one that is comfortable for you but does not weigh too much. I have recently started to use as Adamo ISM saddle which once I got used too has been amazing. Speak to your local dealer and see if they have a sample one you can try before you buy. They really are worth the money and I will be getting one for all of my bikes.

Question No.340
What are the categories of Paratriathlon?

This is a broad subject and it is advisable to visit the ITU's website for the current information regarding this - http://www.triathlon.org/about/downloads_category/paratriathlon. Your national body will have multiple assessment days throughout the year for you to attend. These generally take an hour.

Question No.341
What should be my first point of contact to get into PT?

Speak to your local triathlon club to find out what they offer and if they have an established section for Paratritahlon. If not then contact your national Triathlon Association for advice on a club near you.

Question No.342
Do all races have to let me compete or can they refuse too?

There is no reason why you should be refused entry to a race. If you are and it is sanctioned by your national body, then contact them for advice.

Question No.343
Am I able to have assistance if needed?

Yes - an allowance is made for you to have assistance. Event organizers can request a form from their national body to allow them to make changes. Different numbers of helpers are allowed depending on which category you are racing in.

Question No.344
What happens if I get a puncture on the bike and cannot repair it?

You should be able to seek assistance in this instance.

Question No.345
Are the Paratriathlon only races?

Yes - contact your national body for advice.

Question No.346
How old do I have to be to compete?

You need to be 16 to compete in adult competirion.

Question No.347
Is there any specialist coaching available for Paratriathletes?

In the UK there are 9 regional coaches who specialize in paratriathlon.

Question No.348
I need a chair - how much do I need to budget for one?

You should budget a similar amount as an able bodied athlete would for a carbon bike. This means that they are expensive so it is advisable to try and gain sponsorship or grants from businesses. The CAF in the USA have grants specifically for this.

Q. No.349
What are the best "Golden Nuggets" of wisdom that you have learnt about Triathlon?

Sleep lots and allow yourself to recover
Have rest days. They are hugely important
Get your nutrition right
Be consistent in your training.
When you think you cannot go any faster then push harder.
Learn to suffer.
Your slow runs are supposed to be slow. Most go way too fast.
Smile!

Q. No.350
What are the most common rules that I need to be aware of?

Please refer to your sanctioning body for a full list of rules but below is a summary of the major ones:-
1. You must wear a helmet on the bike with your chin strap securely fastened.
2. Your helmet must be worn in T1 before you take your bike and must remain on and fastened until you secure yout bike in T2.
3. You are not allowed to draft whilst on the bike. That is to say that you should leave a gap of at least 3 bike lengths to the rider in front unless you are overtaking. When performing an overtaking manouvre you must do so with a set amount of time (usually 15seconds) and do so on the right.
4. You may not seek outside assistance at any time. If you need help then ask a marshal. The only exception of course is if you are ill or injured and in need of assistance.
5. You must not wear headphones at any time during the race.
6. You must act in a sportsmanlike manner.
7. Race numbers must be worn on your back during the bike and at the front for the run.

Q. No.351
Do you have a raceday checklist so I don't forget anything?

Race Day Checklist (this can be downloaded and printed from our website)
Race licence, otherwise you will have to pay a day licence fee.
Bike helmet.
Running and cycling shoes.
Your bike.
Transition box containing anti chafing protection, safety pins, post race drink, race belt, plastic bags, bin liner in case it is raining, sun screen, multi tool, light weight waterproof jacket.
Sunglasses
Lip Balm
Toilet paper
Nutrition
Water bottle
Puncture repair kit
Bike pump
Track pump
Spare inner tubes
Goggles
Swim costume/Tri Suit
Socks and a spare dry pair.
Warm top for before and after the race
ID System
Cycling gloves
Drinks
Cap

Question No.352
I would love to get my kids involved in Triathlon - what is the best way to do this?

Children really are the future of the sport and the more youth triathletes that are involved in the sport the better. Sadly schools in general do not seem to offer triathlon so it is up to parents to motivate, inspire and get their kids involved. It is so good for them and what kid does not like to swim, bike and run naturally? Lets start to motivate the young at grass roots level by letting them join in with us and participate in some of our training. As an added bonus you will have great one on one time with your kids that is not achievable with sports such as football.

Speak to your local triathlon clubs and regional bodies to discover who has a programme in place for youth training.

Question No.353
Are there any pieces of non triathlon specific equipment that I should consider buying?

I love to juice so find a Phillips juicer indispensable. Juicing is a great way to deliver nutrients to you body quickly and effectively. There are many books on the subject but I particularly recommend Jason Vale "The Juice Master" who has written multiple books on the subject and is the world authority on it.

I recently visited some good friends in Italy and they had a Vitamix Total Nutrition System mixer which was quite simply amazing. It is so powerful that it will actually make creamy smooth hot soups from cold ingredients purely through friction caused by the blades power. It is incredibly versatile and powerful and lets you make everything from ice cream to bread dough to scrambled eggs to guacamole to smoothies. This is definitely going to be my next purchase

The article below was written by Sarah Russell who has an MSc in sport science from Brunel University and 18 years experience as a trainer, coach, elite lightweight rower, runner and triathlete.

Running Technique

Has anyone ever actually taught you how to run properly? Shown you the correct technique? Taught you exactly how your feet should hit the ground or what your arms should do? No? Well it's not surprising. It's highly unlikely that you've ever been 'taught' running technique as such and if you're completely honest, you're probably wondering if it's even important. When we think about running, we focus on how many miles to run or how fast to run them, very few of us think about our technique and how to improve it. After all, running isn't exactly a 'technical' sport is it? You simply put one foot in front of the other and do what comes naturally. If we can walk, then surely we can run; and do it in our own 'style', which works for us – so no need to change it.

All you have to do is type 'running technique' into Google however, and you'll see that there are many people who disagree. Running technique or style is becoming a hot topic at the moment and it seems everyone has a different view on what's wrong and right. But it's all getting a bit confusing. There are so many different methods, styles and techniques all promising amazing results, fewer injuries and faster times, that it can be difficult to sort the cowboys from the scientists. Forefoot running is the 'buzzword' of the moment, but is it right for everyone? Does it work for you? How do you do it and most importantly, how do you know when you're getting it right? And what about all the different methodologies and schools of thought? How do they all fit into the jigsaw and are they relevant for you? Here we'll try to put the record straight and give you some simple advice and top tips on becoming a better runner, whether you're a veteran or a newcomer.

What is poor technique?

Lets start by looking at what we mean by an 'inefficient' running style. If you watch the lead runners in a quality road race go past, they make it look effortless. They're not all running in exactly the same way, but they have certain similarities. You can barely hear their feet hit the ground, they look relaxed and simply seem to glide along, despite working extremely hard. As the race progresses, and towards the mid or back of the field, things start to change. You can hear the sound of feet stamping the ground, runners look pained, tense and uncomfortable. People go past with clenched fists, arms locked by their sides, knees knocking, shuffling their feet, making it look so difficult and like they'd much rather be elsewhere. And this is supposed to be fun?! You could argue that elite runners are taught properly, they are 'different' to the rest of us and just genetically 'know' how to run and plus the fact they're about 10kg lighter, which helps. But what's to stop you from adopting a few of their techniques? To put a bit of thought into what your body is doing and try to relax a bit more? You never know, you might well run a bit faster, enjoy it more and dare we say it, look better?

Common running mistakes. Can you recognise any of these faults in yourself or your running partner?

Clenched fists
Scrunched up face
Hunched shoulders
Floppy wrists
Shuffling feet
Toes turned out/ turned in
Leaning too far forwards/backwards
Twisting from side to side
Arms too high/too low
Knees knocking together
Straight arms
Bouncing up and down
Arms flailing around
Heavy foot strike/slapping sound

Ask a friend to take a critical look at your running style based on these points and give you some feedback. Or you could video each other and watch it back to analyse your style.

Running inefficiently means you're wasting energy and not using your body correctly to propel you forwards, as well as potentially risking injury. Take the arms for example. Twisting the shoulders from side to side with the arms swinging across your body means you're propelling your energy sideways, not forwards, which is where you're trying to go. Meaning you'll a) run less efficiently and b) have unnecessary tension in your shoulders and arms. The simple action of tucking in your elbows and thinking about a 'forwards and backwards' motion instead with the arms can be enough to get your arms behaving properly and means you'll propel yourself forwards in the direction you're aiming to go.

Top tip
When you're out running, make it a habit to do a 'form check' every 5 minutes or so. Especially towards the end of a race.. it helps take your mind off the pain and gives you focus.

What about injuries?

Our biomechanics often adapt following an injury or after years of muscle imbalances and weakness. Those knock-knees for example could be a symptom of weak glutes and pelvic instability. When the glutes aren't firing correctly to stabilise the pelvis, the ITB and piriformus are called into action and end up overcompensating, pulling the knee in across the midline in a valgus position. In some cases this is relatively minor and not visible to the naked eye, in other cases it's very obvious and can be observed when running behind someone. In time this could potentially lead to knee pain or ITB syndrome, especially if your mileage increases. So interestingly your sore 'runners knee' might not be anything to do with your knee at all, but a symptom of your weak glutes and instable pelvis.

'The body is a kinetic chain' explains Mike Antoniades of The Running School in Chiswick, London (www.runningschool.co.uk) 'and your muscular and skeletal systems all work together when you run. You simply can't isolate one muscle group or body part from the other, they are all linked in a kinetic chain relying on each other and compensating for weakness or problems elsewhere. Take the feet for example. 'There is too much focus on gait analysis from the knee down' he says 'often what the feet are doing is indicative of a problem higher up the chain and simply prescribing 'motion control' shoes for example isn't enough. Shoe choice is only part of the picture and we should be looking at the whole body to assess the problems and look at how to fix them.'

Mitchell Phillips of StrideUK in Brighton agrees 'you can't just say 'I've now decided to start running but am going to stop my feet from turning out.' When in fact the problem is highly likely to be in your back or pelvis, which is causing you to run like that. By trying to change your style and trying to run with your toes forced into neutral instead will increase muscle resistance and simply throw out problems elsewhere. What we do at StrideUK is identify the cause of the problem and work on a series of strengthening, stretching and rebalancing exercises which will mean the feet start to return to neutral on their own'.

If you've been running for many years, your style and associated problems will be more ingrained. Suddenly changing your technique overnight is a) virtually impossible to do and b) likely to have you sidelined with an injury. So the answer is to make gradual changes to improve your general 'running form', and try to simply become more aware of what your body is doing.   You can make basic changes to your running form, but if you have significant biomechanical problems due to an old injury or a muscle imbalance, you need to get assessed, identify the problem and work both technique and re-balancing your body with the right exercises and drills.

What is good technique?

Running efficiently and with 'good form' just feels better and you'll soon know when you're running well and getting it right. With more body awareness and better mind/body dialogue you'll be able to correct your inefficiencies during a run and refocus when you feel your technique start to deteriorate. But is it really that simple? And how do you run with 'good technique'?

Here are a few of our top tips for good running form

1. Think about your arms as 'pistons' by your side. Avoid twisting and aim for a 'forwards and backwards' motion. Your elbow should be a relaxed 90 degree angle and your arm should swing from the shoulder. Aim to drive back with the elbows instead of reaching forwards with the hands.

2. Hands should feel relaxed but with 'firm' wrists. Avoid clenching

your fists. Imagine you're holding a 'crisp' between your thumb and forefinger – and try not to break it!

3. Shoulders should be relaxed, shoulder blades pulled back and chest lifted.

4. Heel striking causes a 'braking effect' and increases the amount of force transmitted through your body, whereas mid or fore foot running is more efficient and effective, propelling you onto the next step more easily. You can't (nor shouldn't) try to become a mid foot runner overnight though, but what you can do is reduce the braking effect. Your legs should do a 'cycling' action underneath you, leading with the knee (not heel) and landing with a slightly bent knee.

5. Relax your face and jaw, (some runners grind their teeth or chew their tongues) – especially in a tough race or session.

6. Relax your whole body. Tension wastes energy.

7. Lean slightly forwards, but not excessively. You should aim to land with your foot just under your centre of gravity – not in front of your body.

8. Try to land lightly to run smoothly and efficiently without any 'up and down' movement of the body.

9. When the foot leaves the ground, try to make sure the heel moves up towards the buttock to engage the hamstring and glute muscles. This shortens the stride and increases cadence.

According to Mike Antoniades, good running technique can be taught and involves not just the body, but the mind too. He believes that the nervous, muscular, skeletal and cardiovascular systems of the body are all involved when we run, and we can improve the biomechanics of our running style, by getting all these systems to work in partnership with each other. 'We have designed modules to teach athletes how to run faster and more effectively as well as how to avoid common sports and running injuries' says Mike 'Many of us have never been taught how to run. We think its something that we pick-up naturally and we don't realize until the pain begins that we are actually running inefficiently which can lead to injuries'.

Mitchell at StrideUK says 'Video Gait Analysis proves the best test of all times… seeing is believing. I have found that the best way to improve your running performance is to see exactly how your body copes every step of your way. Our 360degree systems do just that. It's also important to recognise that we all run differently, after all, we're all built differently, and with that to mind, we all react differently. We at StrideUK believe there is no one particular running style for all. It's all about understanding your limitations and building a style best tailored around that. We'll work on reducing the negatives, and increase the positives!'

Try this:
The next time you go out running, try to be a little more aware of what your body is doing. Where are your hands? Are your shoulders hunched up? Do you land on your heel or midfoot? Do your shoulders twist from side to side? Becoming more aware of your body and getting more in tune with it is the first step to being a faster and more efficient runner. Once you're aware of your weakness in your running style, give yourself some cues to work on the problems. Positive cues like 'relax hands' or 'lift chest' or 'shoulders back' can make all the difference.. repeat them in your head or out loud if you feel your technique deteriorating.

Newton Shoes
Newton running shoes are designed to 'encourage' you onto your fore foot and aim to make you a more efficient and faster runner. According to Mike Trees (UK importer of Newton shoes and former Masters 10,000m World Champion) the original Newton (Gravity and Motion) are most suitable for those people who currently run mid/fore foot or for people who are serious about making a fast transition. Just putting on a pair of traditional Newton's will not turn you into a 'fore foot' runner overnight as the transition requires an adaptation period. To make Newton shoes more widely available to a broader market however, and therefore more suitable for heavier runners and heel strikers, Newton have recently introduced the new 'Sir and Lady Isaac' model – this is also known as a transition shoe with more cushioning, control and support, for heel strikers aiming to become fore foot runners. To run faster simply by changing your shoes however is an

attractive prospect, and not only do the shoes look (and feel) amazing, the science is there behind them, but just make sure you get advice before buying a pair. To find out more go to www.newtonrunning. co.uk

Final Word

Running technique should not be complicated or confusing. There are things we can all focus on to become more efficient runners and some simple changes to our 'running form' can make all the difference. But try not to over-focus on one particular running technique or method. There is no 'one size fits all' when it come to running technique and there is no such thing as a perfect technique, if there was we'd all run in the same way. There are many varying methods and schools of thought out there, so do your research, get feedback on your own form and simply develop a style that works for you and within your biomechanical limitations and goals.

Below are details of companies that I personally use and recommend. This is always being updated so please visit www.triathlon-questions.com to hear of any new discoveries.

Torq Nutrition - www.torqfitness.co.uk

I first came across Torq at the Triathlon Show in the UK where I was able to sample the nutrition products from multiple companies including all the main brands. To me Torq stood out by far. Previously it had taken me up to 3 miles to eat one energy bar with them being so dry and dense but Torq's were moist, very tasty and edible. The fat content is less than 1gm per 100 (others are up to 8gm) which aids the absorption of energy into your system. You are also able to take in 90gm per hour instead of the usual 60gm which is a revelation for me. I cannot emphasise enough how much Torq have helped me nutrition wise and through their fitness consultancy where I had my lactic threshold measured properly to give me genuine training zones for when I am training on the bike.

Cycle Active - www. cycleactive.com

I am a great believer that building skill sets in complementary sports can be very beneficial. Cycle Active give a range of Mountain Bike courses around the UK and to my mind are excellent. I wanted to learn how to handle a MTB better so attended their Level 2 Single-track and Jumps and Drops courses. I truly learnt an amazing amount, built my confidence up and really improved my bike handling skills which transfer over to my road cycling. By being a more competent MTBer I am now able to spend hours exploring the countryside away from traffic .

Virgin Active - www.virginactive.com

Virgin Active have gyms located around the world and I want to support them as they support Triathlon by holding the World's largest triathlon in London each year. Their gyms offer a safe place to train during the harsh winters with excellent trainers and lots of classes, internal competitions and friendly, knowledgeable staff.

Penny's Personal Training - www.pennystraining.com

Penny is my personal trainer who I use to ensure I am using the correct form when strength training and for motivation. Having a trainer need not be expensive and I only see Penny a few times a year as I find it stops bad habits forming and keeps me on track. Penny runs a selection of group exercises that are suitable for all levels and especially mums getting back into fitness. She is super friendly and an excellent runner and triathlete herself.

Ben Wright - www.ben-efit.co.uk

Ben is the owner of Ben-E-Fit personal training and specializes in cycling being a ex-pro himself. I am lucky to have Ben as one of the Maidstone Harriers Tri club coaches. Even though I have ridden a bike all my life I have learnt a wealth of information from Ben which has really transformed my cycling ability.

Giovanna Richards - www.bluemantaswimming.com

Like a number of Triathletes, swimming is a weak point for me so it was a revelation to take tuition from "G". She is one of the top open water coaches in the country and has many weekly pool based Master Sessions. Since using "G" my swim times have improved considerably.

Mark Dayson - www.mdp-physio.co.uk

Mark Dayson MCSP ACPSEM PG Dip

Mark is the physiotherapist leading Dayson Physio & Sports Rehab / MDP Physio and works with athletes and the general public in two locations in Kent and across multiple locations for teams and clubs. He offers a full assessment and treatment of sports injuries and all musculoskeletal injuries, utilising maual therapy electrotherapy, sports massage, kinesio taping and excercise rehabilitation. There is also full athlete screening for clubs, individuals and teams from basic to advanced. He also delivers workshops on a range of subjects related to injury prevention and conditioning to all sports.

Mark is the physiotherapist for England Basketball U14 & U15 Boys Team having recently toured with the team to Newcastle/Scotland and Copenhagen

Mark also offers assessment and treatment for endurance athletes inclusive of coaching and planning and periodisation of training. Analysis of running style are offered with corrective coaching and conditioning coming from a background as an athlete for 14 years and UK Athletics Endurance Coach for 10 years. Educational seminars are available for recreational runners, groups, leaders, coaches and clubs

Mark is also the physiotherapeutic lead for the Advanced Apprenticeship in Sporting Excellence at The Canterbury Academy covering athletics, basketball, dance, gymnastics, football (Chelsea FC Academy @ Canterbury), rugby, squash, tennis and trampolining. Screening, assessment and treatment and prehab, rehab and post rehab in conjunction with Steve Green, Academy lead on S&C

Sarah Russell - www.sarahsrunners.co.uk
Sarah has over 20 years experience as a running coach, personal trainer and fitness expert. She has represented Great Britain as an U23 lightweight rower in 1993, and more recently as part of Team GB at the European and World Duathlon Championships in 2006 and 2007. She is a qualified running coach (CiRF) and holds a UKA coach license as well as an MSc in Sport Science from Brunel University. She is a freelance Health and Fitness writer, writing monthly for Running Fitness Magazine and Nuffield Health. She is currently the Race Director for the award winning Tunbridge Wells Half Marathon. She also runs a group called "Sarah's Runners" which has around 350 members.

Matt Atwell at NRP - www.naturalrunningproject.com
I am indebted to Matt who transformed my running. I used to be a heel striker until Matt analyzed my running style and recommended that I change to a mid foot strike. This has not only made me a lot faster but as also kept injury away. The Natural Running Project is a formidable team.

Adamo - www.ismseat.com
Like a number of cyclist my rear can get a little sore if spending a prolonged time in the saddle. I was eager to try the Adamo ISM range of saddles for their added comfort. They do take some time to adjust to but once set up properly they are a revelation and offer real all day comfort.

Wyndy Milla - www.wyndymilla.com
I ride a Wyndy Milla "Massive Attack" which is an awesome bike that I love. Not only is it amazingly fast it is also pretty unique and easily found in transition. It receives all sorts of complements from those in the know and is fantastic to ride. If you are after a custom bike that the pros use then Wyndy Milla has to be your choice.

Flying Fox Bikes - www.flyingfoxbikes.com

I used Flying Fox bikes when I purchased my Lapierre Mountain Bike. I have not visited yet but believe there is great riding to be had around the shop.

Garmin - www.garmin.com

I really cannot see why anyone would use any other GPS device for training or racing. I use a Edge 810 and 910 XT and find them indispensable.

Alert ID - www.alertid.co.uk

I personally believe that an Alert ID is an absolute must for anyone who participates in sports. If you are involved in an accident or get injured an Alert ID will enable the emergency services to find out who you are, any medical conditions you have and inform your family of which hospital you are in. They are very inexpensive and could literally save your life.

www.velominati.com/the-rules/

I love reading through "The Rules" and forgive them for Rule #42.

NOTES